THE GREAT BOOK OF ROCK TRIVIA

Amazing Trivia, Fun Facts & The History of Rock and Roll

BY

Bill O'Neill

ISBN-13:978-1724747068

CONTENTS

INTRODUCTION

Rock music is the soundtrack to many of our lives. We remember our first concert, the songs we danced to in high school, and scouring magazines for news of our favorite singers. Psychologists present several reasons we're interested in celebrities: schadenfreude, wanting to be like them, fantasy, or just wanting something to talk about with friends. Whatever your desire, this book will give you some extraordinary facts about your favorite musicians. But that's not all. You'll also learn the stories behind some of the best rock songs! Plus, you'll find fascinating details about some of the most exciting and momentous concerts, as well as the origins of rock and roll and its evolution through the years.

Read on and learn about the rock musicians who helped build the hippie counterculture of the 1960s, with the rallying call of "sex, drugs, and rock and roll" and the idealism shining through the Summer of Love and culminating in Woodstock. Then the '70s came, and rock music shifted from the counterculture to seat itself firmly in mainstream culture, and it became more capitalistic. There was money to be made in music! The Beatles fans of the '60s were adults with cash to spend. Record companies and radio stations started labeling different forms of rock music so fans could find and buy it more easily: progressive rock, acid or psychedelic rock, heavy metal, folk rock and, later, disco and punk.

Learn about bands like Led Zeppelin, who pioneered heavy blues and gave us hard rock and heavy metal. Rockers' attention-grabbing antics expanded from Elvis's provocative dancing and the Who's instrument smashing, to excesses with substances and groupies. Increasingly outlandish (and gender-bending) clothing and makeup, and occultish images (the latter were most often part of a band's gimmick and not necessarily reflective of a musician's actual beliefs or practices). Grunge emerged as a reaction to glam rock and became the preferred genre for '90s youth.

This book will take you through the rock stars who shaped rock history through all these years. You'll learn which heavy metal monster now coaches Little League. Find out who had an adventure with an exorcist and which band is secretly made up of self-described book nerds! Learn how rock stars and Hare Krishnas were connected and which superstar won the same award eight years in a row.

Find loads of rock trivia to impress your co-workers and friends in seven fun-filled chapters, starting with the roots of rock and roll. Learn about the superstars, the bands, the hit songs, and some unforgettable concert experiences. Read about the awards musicians have won and the records they (and their fans!) have broken. Which Beatle inspired the most novelty songs? (It's probably not the one you're thinking of!) Which country's former president led a revolution because of a local band? Each chapter has a quiz at the end as an extra challenge. Now get on your magic carpet ride or magic bus and come with us!

CHAPTER ONE
BACK TO THE BEGINNING

Every story has a beginning. The early history of rock and roll music is as complex as a good guitar riff, and with just as many variations. From African American blues musicians to the first electric guitar and the phrase "rock and roll," rock became a revolutionary musical form for American youth and spread to people of all ages worldwide. But rock and roll continued to evolve. Who was the first band to play psychedelic rock? When (and why) did male rock stars start keeping long hair? Read on for the "famous firsts" in rock music.

Why Do We Call It That?

Where did the term "rock and roll" come from? The oldest known usage of the phrase depicts the movements of a ship at sea. Later, people used it to describe spiritual rapture in churches, the motion of a train, dancing, and sexual activity.

Alan Freed was the first person to refer to a type of music as rock and roll, in 1951. A disc jockey in Cleveland, Ohio, he played R&B songs on his late-night program, "Moondog Rock 'n' Roll Party." He felt that the phrase "rock 'n' roll" aptly illustrated the beat of the music.

Soon after this, still-segregated America began to differentiate between rock and roll performed by whites and by African Americans, calling the latter "rhythm and blues," or "R&B." This distinction was fluid, however, and there has never been universal agreement on what is and what isn't rock and roll. The Rock and Roll Hall of Fame, for example, has inducted a number of artists that would have been called R&B in the '50s.

The Face of Rock and Roll

Most of the well-known rock musicians today are white, but the founders of rock and roll were not. In the 1989 film *Great Balls of Fire*, Jerry Lee Lewis stands outside an African American club, watching Big Maybelle perform "Whole Lotta Shakin' Goin' On." We all know the rest—the song was one of his greatest hits!

But Big Maybelle, a black woman, performed it first, in 1955. What we today call rock music emerged as a hybrid of country, blues, gospel, and jazz, among others, and the earliest performers of most of these genres were African Americans.

Sister Rosetta Tharpe was a black woman who sang both gospel and rock. She accompanied herself on the electric guitar, shredding it as well as, if not better than, any male performer (it was uncommon for a woman to play the guitar in the '30s and '40s). Her 1963 performance in England was a huge influence on later British rock guitarists, including Eric Clapton and Keith Richards.

Other black pioneers of rock and roll include Fats Domino, Ray Charles, Ike Turner, and Lloyd Price.

The First Rock and Roll Record

No one can agree on the first rock and roll record, probably because no one can agree on the borders of rock and roll. In 2004, *Rolling Stone* magazine claimed that Elvis Presley's "That's All Right Mama" was the first rock record. Others consider Bill Haley to be the first who successfully synthesized R&B and country into rock to create "Rock Around the Clock." Most music scholars today argue that neither of these artists produced the first rock and roll record.

While Elvis released "That's All Right Mama" in 1954, one of his idols, Arthur Crudup, had recorded it in 1946. Other contenders for the title of first rock record include Goree Carter's "Rock Awhile" (1949), "Good Rocking Tonight," recorded by both Roy Brown (1947) and Wynonie Harris (1948), and Sister Rosetta Tharpe's "Strange Things Happening Every Day," recorded way back in 1944.

Though the vote is far from unanimous, the song most commonly cited as the first rock record is "Rocket 88" by Ike Turner. While most of us know Ike as Tina Turner's ex-husband, he had his own band, Kings of Rhythm, as early as the late '40s. "Rocket 88," like many rock songs after it, was about a car—an Oldsmobile. Turner and the Kings of Rhythm recorded the song in 1951, with saxophonist Jackie Brenston providing the vocals.

Who Invented the Electric Guitar?

If there's one thing that's essential in rock music, it's wielding the axe. Where would rock music be without the electric guitar? With a few exceptions, such as Jerry Lee Lewis, who accompanied himself on the piano, rock groups have used the electric guitar to create those characteristic power chords, reverb effects, and fuzz tones. But where did it come from?

Like the invention of rock, it's complicated. The first known person to electrify a guitar was George Breed, an officer in the U.S. Navy. Unfortunately, it didn't go anywhere, but considering it was 1890, it's a pretty impressive accomplishment. Lloyd Loar, an employee of Gibson, built an electric bass and an electric viola in 1924. While Gibson is a big name in electric guitars today, they manufactured non-electric banjos and mandolins in the '20s, and Loar left the company to start his own.

A company called Stromberg-Voisinet advertised electric guitars in 1929, but they may not have actually produced them. In 1931, Adolph Rickenbacker and George Beauchamp teamed up to design the "Frying Pan," an electric steel guitar. The award for "first mass-produced electric guitar" may belong to them, and the Rickenbacker brand still produces electric guitars today.

Electric guitars were invented to solve a problem—the sound of acoustic guitars gets lost in a large, loud orchestra. It was only later that musicians and manufacturers discovered all the cool things they could do with an electric guitar. For example, Grady Martin, bassist to Marty Robbins, ended up with a "fuzz tone" when his amplifier malfunctioned while performing "Don't Worry About Me." They liked the sound, and it's now a standard feature.

The British Are Coming!

The British invasion, while not so good for the American musicians it displaced, was a welcome antidote for a nation mourning the assassination of a beloved president. The novelty of artists such as the Beatles, the Animals, Petula Clark, the Kinks, and Herman's Hermits delighted young audiences and helped lift the nation's spirits.

The first British band to tour the U.S. was the Dave Clark Five. Their music featured a harder drum sound than their peers, and the other band members—and the audience—often amplified the beat by stomping their feet. As a result, some venues forbade the DC5 from performing their drum-heaviest song, "Bits and Pieces." Drummer Dave Clark was used to a little danger, though. He was a stunt man in his teens!

The Rolling Stones and the Who took a bit longer than the Beatles and the DC5 to find success with an American audience. The Stones were the "bad boys," in contrast to the Beatles at that time. Even so, the lead singer is now *Sir* Mick Jagger after being knighted in 2003. Guitarist Keith Richards accused Jagger of "selling out" by accepting the knighthood. The Stones were among the first performers to wear long hair, and some of Mick Jagger's hair was sold for $6,000 in 2013.

Before they were the Beatles, the fab four called themselves the Blackjacks, and then the Quarrymen. The famous "mop top" haircut first crowned Stu Sutcliffe, an early member who left the Beatles in 1961. His hair was styled by Astrid Kirchherr, a German photographer he had a romantic relationship with, and it soon caught on with the rest of the band—except for drummer Pete Best, whose curly hair wouldn't sit that way. And speaking of which...

What's With That Hair?

Even Elvis's pompadour (he was naturally blond, by the way) was seen as rebellious in the '50s, and a teenager was suspended from school for wearing his hair in the "Elvis" style. Adults linked unconventional hair (and a taste for rock music) to poor academic performance. As the rock era progressed, however, hair got longer as youth rebelled against a culture created by adults who favored hair barely longer than military style.

Southern rock band Lynyrd Skynyrd named themselves after Leonard Skinner, a high school P.E. teacher who gave the band members hell for wearing long hair. Guitarist Gary Rossington ended up dropping out of school in frustration with the dress code. Mr. Skinner later introduced the band at a concert.

The now-dreaded mullet rose in popularity in the '70s and '80s, sported by Rod Stewart, David Bowie, and lead singer of Def Leppard Joe Elliot. However, this "business in the front, party in the back" hairstyle was not called the mullet until 1994, when the Beastie Boys released "Mullet Head."

In the '90s, long hair was no longer seen as rebellious and a must-have for rock musicians. Many formerly long-haired rockers such as Jon Bon Jovi and all the members of Metallica cut theirs. Still, some of Metallica's fans worried that the band was softening its image.

A Rock and Roll Magazine

While the Rolling Stones formed part of the British Invasion, a different *Rolling Stone* came out of San Francisco, California. Founder Jann Wenner published the first issue of the rock music magazine in 1967 out of a loft apartment. In fact, the staff was so small that many articles appeared without bylines. Wenner didn't want readers to know that the magazine had so few writers.

The first cover featured John Lennon in the military uniform he wore in the film *How I Won the War*. In fact, Lennon graced the cover 30 times, either alone, with the Beatles, or with Yoko Ono. Annie Leibovitz took the iconic photo of John Lennon curled up naked next to a clothed Yoko Ono hours before he died on

December 8, 1980. That photo appeared on the cover the following month.

While a single issue of *Rolling Stone* currently sells for $6.99 on store shelves, the first issue cost only 25¢. Hunter S. Thompson's book *Fear and Loathing in Las Vegas* first appeared as a story in *Rolling Stone*. Cameron Crowe's movie *Almost Famous* was inspired by his time writing for the magazine.

Psychedelic Rock

The fact that recreational drug use was prevalent in the '60s is the subject of many jokes, and many people link rock music— and musicians—to drug use. That's not always the case, as there are several rock musicians who don't use them. The list of drug-free rockers includes Adam Ant, Bruce Springsteen, Angus Young of AC/DC, Ian Anderson of Jethro Tull, and Gene Simmons, the lead singer of KISS. What's more, these five musicians don't even drink alcohol. That's right: Gene Simmons was *sober* onstage behind all the fake blood and makeup!

Psychedelic rock, however, used music to recreate the mind-altering effects of LSD for the listener—whether or not the musician actually composed or performed the song while under the influence. The Grateful Dead even flashed strobe lights during their performances to enhance the experience.

One of the first (many say *the* first) and most influential psychedelic rock songs was "Eight Miles High" by the Byrds, an

American band that loved the Beatles. Banned in some parts of the U.S. due to the double meaning of the word "high," the song describes the band's first airplane trip to London. In an odd twist, one of the song's writers left the band shortly afterward due to a fear of flying. The guitar riffs were inspired by John Coltrane's composition "India."

Many psychedelic rock songs contained explicit drug references—or did they? John Lennon wrote "Lucy in the Sky" after seeing a picture his young son, Julian, had drawn. Peter, Paul and Mary's hit "Puff the Magic Dragon" describes the end of childhood. And one night, Jimi Hendrix went to bed after reading a sci-fi story and had a strange dream that resulted in "Purple Haze." And "Incense and Peppermints" by Strawberry Alarm Clock? Well...that one's about marijuana.

RANDOM FUN FACTS

1. Actually, the title of "first rock star" goes to 19th century Hungarian composer and pianist Franz Liszt. His good looks, long hair, and flamboyant performances inspired "Lisztomania" in Europe, and women stormed the stage to rip off scraps of his clothing and collect strands of his hair.

2. Ritchie Valens (Richard Valenzuela) was the first Mexican American rock star. His smash hit "La Bamba" was originally a folk song from the Mexican state of Veracruz. It was traditionally performed at weddings, and the bride and groom had to work together to tie a bow with their feet.

3. Jerry Lee Lewis was the first rock star to destroy musical instruments onstage. He once pushed a piano off the stage, and he lit another one on fire.

4. Little Richard's drummer claims they were the first (male) band to wear eyeshadow and earrings. While "Tutti Frutti" remains one of the most influential rock songs, its original lyrics had to be rewritten due to explicit sexual references.

5. Before he was a rock star, Chuck Berry was a hairdresser. He became famous for his witty word play (rock lyrics were quite simple and repetitive at that time), even referencing classical musicians in "Roll Over Beethoven."

6. George Harrison was one of the first performers to play the sitar in a rock song. The instrument featured prominently in "Norwegian Wood."

7. Dr. Hook & the Medicine Show, of "The Cover of 'Rolling Stone'" fame, finally did get their pictures on the cover of *Rolling Stone*—in cartoon form, and captioned with "What's-Their-Names Make the Cover." Satire goes both ways.

8. Elvis and Liberace were friends, and it was that flamboyant pianist who suggested that Elvis fancy up his stage wardrobe.

9. There are different techniques musicians use to create a fuller sound in the finished studio recording. Although they didn't invent it, Les Paul (yes, the guitar guy) and Mary Ford were the ones who brought multitrack recording into rock music.

10. Another technique was ADT—automatic, or artificial, double-tracking. This combined an original recording with a delayed copy. The Beatles were the first to use this technique. John was particularly interested in double-tracking his vocals, and he asked their recording engineer to develop a new technique for the band.

11. Vinyl records are wonderful, but you can't really listen to them in the car. Hence, the 8-track player was born. The

Ford Motor Company was the first to offer 8-track players in cars, in 1965.

12. Japanese businessman Daisuke Inoue used an 8-track player to invent the first karaoke machine, in 1971.

13. And then there were cassette tapes. Some of the first musicians on cassette were Eartha Kitt, Nina Simone, and Johnny Mathis, in 1966.

14. The first album on CD is a draw: The first commercial CD produced, in 1982, was ABBA's *The Visitors*, but *52nd Street* by Billy Joel was available for sale before ABBA's CD was.

15. Electric guitars are made with more than just electricity. They rely on electromagnetism to produce the currents.

16. Before rock musicians adopted the electric guitar, it was favored by country, blues, and jazz musicians.

17. The first British musician to have a No. 1 hit on the American pop charts was not who you're thinking of: It was a jazz clarinetist named Mr. Acker Bilk, and his instrumental hit was called "Stranger on the Shore."

18. A number of British invasion bands, such as the Beatles, were from Liverpool, and their sound was nicknamed "Merseybeat" back in England, after the river that runs through Liverpool.

19. Elvis Presley, Jerry Lee Lewis, Johnny Cash, Carl Perkins, and

Roy Orbison all started on the same record label: Sun Records.

20. The "fuzz guitar" sound on "Rocket 88" was originally unintentional. An amplifier was damaged and guitarist Willie Kizart stuffed crumpled newspapers inside it to hold the cone in place.

TEST YOURSELF – QUESTIONS AND ANSWERS

1. Before becoming the lead singer of the Rolling Stones, Mick Jagger worked at a:

   A) Car dealership

   B) Mental hospital

   C) Bed and breakfast

2. Which of these bands/artists is *not* British?

   A) Frankie Valli and the Four Seasons

   B) The Yardbirds

   C) Dusty Springfield

3. Which early rock star was an avid chess player?

   A) Elvis Presley

   B) Ray Charles

   C) Chuck Berry

4. A subgenre of rock music with strong country roots, usually performed by white singers, including Elvis, Johnny Cash, and Jerry Lee Lewis, was known as:

   A) Bluegrass

   B) Hard Bop

   C) Rockabilly

5. Chuck Berry's hit song "Maybellene" is about:

A) A wedding

B) A car race

C) Big Maybelle

ANSWERS

1. B
2. A
3. B
4. C
5. B

CHAPTER TWO
THE SUPERSTARS

Some names are so big they stand alone. Stars like Elvis Presley, Bob Dylan, and Tina Turner have faces, names, and songs that are recognized everywhere. But they are more than just names; they are people who have lived fascinating lives, full of adventure, loves and losses, successes and failures, and funny stories. Learn some fun facts about your favorite stars!

Elvis Presley

No list would be complete without the King! As beloved as he is today, he was picked on in school, especially for his dyed and immaculately styled hair. The South was strictly segregated when Elvis was a child, but he often spent time in black neighborhoods, listening to black musicians.

Elvis starred in 33 movies, but he didn't like all of them. His favorite was *King Creole*, which he made just before his time in the army. He almost accepted the role of Tony in West Side Story, opposite his former girlfriend Natalie Wood, but his manager talked him out of it.

Elvis loved karate so much he co-founded the Tennessee Karate

Institute, where he earned a seventh-degree black belt. Speaking of black, do you remember the 1989 song "Black Velvet," sung by Alannah Myles? It's about Elvis. When the Chilean miners were trapped in the San Jose mine, they passed the time by singing Elvis songs, led by Edison Peña.

Former Japanese Prime Minister Junichiro Koizumi is another huge Elvis fan. When he visited the U.S., then-President George W. Bush took him to Graceland, becoming the first sitting U.S. president to visit. Other famous Elvis fans include Boris Yeltsin, Eddie Murphy, Dick Clark, and a slew of fellow musicians.

Little Richard

Born Richard Wayne Penniman, he was known for his flamboyant style and daring lyrics. He had 12 siblings and was born with one leg shorter than the other. After a few years of performing, he stopped his career to attend Bible college in 1957. He did return to music a few years later and was a mentor to the Rolling Stones and the Beatles. He vacillated between the church and rock music for decades.

Most people know that Bruce Willis and Demi Moore used to be married, but did you know that Little Richard performed their wedding? Though he has been a vegetarian for over 50 years, he's starred in commercials for Taco Bell and McDonalds. In one Taco Bell commercial, he plays a pink piano on top of a white limousine, sporting an orange jacket and a curly mullet.

Little Richard has appeared on *The Muppet Show* and *Sesame Street*, most notably in 1993, when he sang a rock version of "Rubber Duckie." He sat at the piano, with a bathtub arranged around him so that it looked like he was having a bath, and bubbles floated around him as he sang and played in a jaguar-print jacket. He released an album of children's music in 1992.

Buddy Holly

Buddy Holly had 20/800 vision, but his horn-rimmed glasses made him stand out from other rock stars and also started a trend. His real name was Charles Hardin Holley ("Holly" was originally a typo, but he liked it). He grew up in segregated Texas but, like many other early white rockers, he associated with black musicians. He had a cat named Booker T.

He was one of the first rock stars to write his own material. This inspired other musicians, such as the Beatles, to do the same. Holly's band was called the Crickets. You can hear some real crickets, which had hidden in the studio, at the end of "Listen To Me." John, Paul, George, and Stu, liking the "insect" theme and being big fans of Buddy Holly, finally settled on "the Beatles" for their name.

Holly proposed to Maria Elena Santiago on their first date and married her two months later. His manager advised him to keep his marriage secret to avoid disappointing his female fans. He was a star for less than two years before he died in 1959, but he made it onto *Rolling Stone*'s "100 Greatest Artists," ranking at an impressive number 13, just after the Beach Boys. He also has five songs on the magazine's list "500 Greatest Songs of All Time." At number 499 (or 497, depending on the year) of the same list, Buddy Holly appears again—as the name of a 1994 song by American alternative rock band Weezer.

Bob Dylan

Robert Allen Zimmerman performed as Elston Gunn for a short time before he legally changed his name to Bob Dylan. He once memorized all the songs of civil rights singer Odetta. Her work inspired him to become a folk singer him

. He once played harmonica to accompany another legend— Harry Belafonte.

Dylan is a painter and designed the cover art for two of his albums. He has a taste for difficult literature; his three favorite novels are *Moby Dick*, *All Quiet on the Western Front*, and *The Odyssey*. He was also a fan of Elvis Presley and Charlie Chaplin. Dylan didn't speak for a week after hearing of Elvis's death, and he uses his hat like a prop in the same way Chaplin did.

Bob Dylan's lyrics are the subject of a game between five Swedish scientists: They compete to see who can quote the most Dylan lyrics in their academic papers. It's hard to link Bob Dylan to Nitrate and neurons. One also doesn't readily connect Bob Dylan and women's underwear, but he appeared in a commercial for Victoria's Secret opposite Brazilian model Adriana Lima.

Jimi Hendrix

Neil Young called him "absolutely the best guitar player that ever lived," and who are we to argue with Neil Young? Jimi Hendrix was so good on the guitar that he could play both left and right handed. He did not read music and was self-taught. He may have had synesthesia—he associated chords with colors. The "purple" E7 chord is called the "Hendrix chord" among guitarists.

Hendrix has a star on the Hollywood Walk of Fame, as well as a spot in the Native American Music Hall of Fame. He had some Cherokee blood from his mother's side. He was a big fan of sci-fi literature.

Jimi opened for the Monkees, performed with Cream, and once played guitar for his friend Engelbert Humperdinck. To preserve his "bad boy" image, he stayed behind a curtain while accompanying Humperdinck's orchestra. His song "Voodoo Chile" inspired Dave Murray to learn guitar as a child, and Murray later became the guitarist of Iron Maiden.

Carlos Santana

Carlos Santana's father was a Mariachi musician, and he taught young Carlos to play guitar and violin. The family moved from Mexico to San Francisco, California when Santana was a child. Santana is known as a virtuoso guitarist, but the percussion used in his band, also called Santana, gives the music a distinctive sound as well. The percussion section includes congas, timbales, and bongos, as well as the standard drum set.

But before he became a professional musician, did you know Santana was a busker on the streets of San Francisco? He also worked as a dishwasher. Santana was a follower of the guru Sri Chinmoy at one time, but he decided to leave because the guru tried to forbid Santana and his wife from having children. The Santanas then had three children, the eldest of which, Salvador, is a musician today.

Santana collaborated with John Coltrane's widow, Alice, a multi-instrumentalist herself, to produce *Illuminations*, which featured avant-garde and Indian elements. With his ex-wife Deborah, he runs a charity for children called the Milagro Foundation. Santana is also a restaurant owner. Named after his '90s hit song "Maria Maria," the restaurants serve upscale Mexican food.

Janis Joplin

Janis Joplin was a sensitive person. She was bullied in school and college for her looks and unconventional tastes, causing her to drop out of college. She was never able to forget the experience, and it may have contributed to her hard drug and drinking habits. An advantage of her sensitivity was her ability to connect with her audience emotionally.

She fronted a few different bands, the last one being the Full Tilt Boogie Band. One of her idols was blues queen Bessie Smith, who had died in 1937 and was buried in an unmarked grave. Joplin paid for a gravestone for her. She was not a materialistic person, but one indulgence was a Porsche, painted in colorful psychedelic patterns, which she liked to drive fast on Sunset Blvd.

She also had a lynx fur coat, but that was a gift from the Southern Comfort Company, in gratitude for their product's placement in so many of her photographs. Joplin also used a bottle of Southern Comfort to whack Jim Morrison over the head when he got a little too persistent (and, evidently, it only made him like her more). If she hadn't been in a car, the bottle may have been unnecessary—Joplin had a third-degree black belt in Kenpo Karate!

Although tattoos still raised eyebrows at that time, Janis had two of them. This may have boosted their popularity. After Joplin's death, her ashes were scattered in the Pacific Ocean. Leonard Cohen composed a song about her—"Chelsea Hotel #2." Another tribute to her was Jerry Garcia's "Birdsong." *The Rose*, starring Bette Midler, is a fictional story based on Janis's life.

Patti Smith

The Godmother of Punk almost became the lead singer of Blue Öyster Cult. She wrote the lyrics to several of their songs. The horse brooch that appears on the cover of her album *Horses* was a present from Allen Lanier, Blue Öyster Cult's keyboardist.

Smith is a prolific writer who has published two memoirs: *Just Kids* and *M Train*. She's also published several books of poetry, which she performs. She's currently working on a crime novel. Speaking of crime, she's addicted to TV detective programs, especially the Netflix series *The Killing*. She has a cameo as a doctor in season four.

Patti Smith also loves art. She likes to visit artists' graves and leave things for them. She has also visited Frida Kahlo's house in Mexico. While there, she got a migraine and was invited to rest in Diego Rivera's bed. While in Paris with her sister, before she was a professional musician, she did busking and street performance art.

Smith is active in the Green Party and writes protest music against war, airstrikes, and wrongful incarceration. Her song "About a Boy" is a tribute to the late Kurt Cobain. Other singers have written tributes to Smith too, including Scottish singer KT Tunstall. "Suddenly I See" was inspired by Patti Smith and can be heard at the beginning of the film *The Devil Wears Prada*.

David Bowie

David Bowie was born on Elvis Presley's 12th birthday. His surname was Jones, but he later changed it to avoid being confused with Davy Jones of the Monkees. He could play 14 instruments, including a Japanese stringed instrument called the *koto*. The first one he learned was the saxophone.

Bowie is afraid of heights, but hopefully not rabbits, because a petite individual in a pink bunny costume followed David Bowie around on his 2004 American tour. He never knew who he or she was. David Bowie once became convinced his house was cursed, so he hired an exorcist to take care of the problem. During the exorcism, the swimming pool started bubbling violently.

David Bowie's done a lot of acting. His most famous role was Goblin King Jareth in *Labyrinth*. In one scene, baby Toby sits on Jareth's lap as Jareth whispers in his ear. To keep the baby quiet for the scene, Bowie used a hand puppet (not visible in the clip) to mesmerize the baby (who was the child of the designer).

He also played Andy Warhol in *Basquiat* and Nikola Tesla in *The Prestige*, and did the voice for a character on *SpongeBob SquarePants* called Lord Royal Highness. However, acting can be therapy. For Bowie, performing as Ziggy Stardust was a way to cope with his fear of the mental illness that ran in his family. David Bowie's mime teacher (yes, you read that right) also taught him Kabuki theater performance.

Bowie's hit "Space Oddity," about the out-of-luck astronaut Major Tom, was performed on board the International Space Station. Commander Chris Hadfield sang and played the guitar to the famous song in 2013, but reposted it online after David Bowie's death in 2016. He also has a mile-wide asteroid named after him—342843 Davidbowie is located in an asteroid belt between Mars and Jupiter. A hairy, orange Malaysian spider also bears his name. *Heteropoda davidbowie* measures just under one inch. Folks at Disney are fans too. The giant, gold-plated coconut crab Tamatoa in the animated film *Moana* was inspired by David Bowie, and the crab even has pupils of different sizes!

Tina Turner

Anna Mae Bullock comes from a small town in Tennessee. She had wanted to be a nurse, but she became the Queen of Rock and Roll. When she started performing in Ike Turner's band, she was known as "Little Ann." Her look for the stage was based on comic-book character Sheena, Queen of the Jungle. Former President George W. Bush said Tina Turner's legs were "the most famous in show business."

She holds a Guinness world record for the most concert tickets sold by a solo performer. Aside from her singing career, Tina Turner has acted in a number of films. She was the Acid Queen in the Who's rock opera *Tommy*, but she turned down the role of Shug Avery in *The Color Purple*.

Today, Turner is married to a German music executive and lives in Switzerland. To become a Swiss citizen, she had to pass an advanced German language test. She is also a practicing Buddhist and has met the Dalai Lama. There is a road named "Tina Turner Highway" in her home state of Tennessee.

Bruce Springsteen

Not to be outdone by David Bowie, the Boss has a minor planet named after him: (23990) Springsteen. It is estimated to be two to four kilometers in diameter. Bruce is the frontman of the E Street Band, named for the street the founding keyboardist's mother lived on.

Springsteen is a big baseball fan and, along with members of the E Street Band, challenges local DJs to softball matches while on the road. He also likes taking photos of unusual billboards and signs. When he was young, he once lived near a Nestle factory and could smell the chocolate when the wind was blowing in the right direction.

One of Bruce Springsteen's most notable concerts took place in East Germany in 1988. The socialist government invited him because the youth of the country were fascinated by Western popular music, but journalist Erik Kirschbaum believes the concert inspired East Germans to actively oppose their government. The Berlin Wall came down on 1989.

Joan Jett

Like Springsteen, punk and rock icon Joan Jett loves baseball. She's a big fan of the Baltimore Orioles and has sung the pre-game national anthem for them several times. She also participated in Fantasy Week once, which is an opportunity to be taught baseball by professional coaches just before Spring

Training starts. She's also a fan of the women's basketball team New York Liberty.

Joan Jett has had success with two bands: The Runaways, which she formed at age 15, and Joan Jett & the Blackhearts. The Runaways were much more popular outside the U.S. than at home, and enjoyed an especially enthusiastic reception in Japan. Jett started playing guitar when she was 14 but was annoyed that her instructor kept trying to teach her folk songs.

Jett is played by Kristen Stewart in the movie *The Runaways*, based on bandmate Cherie Currie's memoir. She's a vegetarian and a supporter of PETA and Farm Sanctuary.

Michael Jackson

The King of Pop needs no introduction, and much of his life is common knowledge. But I bet you didn't know that Michael Jackson was a lifelong fan of the Three Stooges and wrote the foreword to Curly's biography! He was also a friend of Stan Lee's and loved Marvel comics. He loved Mexican food too.

"Thriller" is still the most-watched music video of all time. Did you know that the extras needed two weeks of training with the choreographer? Also, Fred Astaire came to one of the rehearsals! Astaire was particularly impressed by Jackson's moonwalk. Jackson's iconic red jacket was padded to make him look bigger, as he only weighed 100 pounds at the time. Horror film actor Vincent Price's lines (you know, the creepy part at the end and the laugh) were a last-minute addition.

Michael Jackson wrote an autobiography called *Moon Walk*. He had some exotic pets: a chimpanzee, two llamas, a ram, a python called Crusher, and a boa constrictor named Muscles. MTV started in 1981, but they didn't play videos by black artists. Jackson's success forced them to play his videos or risk losing viewers. "Billie Jean" was the first video they played by an African-American performer.

Prince

Prince was once known as the Minneapolis Midget because he was only 5'3" and, at the time of his passing, weighed only 112 pounds. He usually wore high-heeled boots to look taller, though this messed up his joints. His height didn't stop him from being good at basketball when he was in school, though!

If you want to write songs like Prince (he wrote over 600), carry a journal with you to jot down ideas like he did. Eating spaghetti with orange juice for dinner, which was his favorite meal, can't hurt either. And say goodbye to your sleep—Prince was known to spend 20 hours recording and even stay awake for days when he was working on something.

Among Prince's many performances, he sang at George Lucas's wedding. Did you know that Michael Jackson's hit "Bad" was supposed to be a duet? Jackson wanted Prince to sing it with him, but Prince objected to the opening line: "Your butt is mine." Especially if Jackson was planning to sing it *to* him.

In 2001, Prince became a Jehovah's Witness. He continued performing, but did not swear or sing songs with sexually explicit lyrics. He gave a lot of money to charities, but did so anonymously, so his generosity was not discovered until after his death. Like Joan Jett, Prince was a vegetarian and an animal rights activist.

Tom Petty

Tom Petty met Elvis when he was ten years old and decided to start a band when he saw the Beatles perform on *The Ed Sullivan Show*. Before becoming a professional musician, he worked as a gravedigger.

He was known for his creative music videos, such as "Don't Come Around Here No More," in which he dresses as the Mad Hatter and cuts up Alice as a cake. He was good friends with singer Stevie Nicks. When Petty's first wife told Nicks that she and Tom had met "at the age of 17," Nicks initially misunderstood and wrote the song "Edge of Seventeen."

Like Bruce Springsteen, Tom Petty and the Heartbreakers performed in concerts with Musicians United for Safe Energy and have a song on the subsequent live album *No Nukes*. He once appeared on *The Simpsons*, teaching Homer to write song lyrics.

Neil Young

Canadian artist Neil Young has several nicknames, and his favorite is Bernard Shakey. He now plays several instruments, but his first was a ukulele. He used to have a hearse nicknamed "Mort" (mortician), which he used to transport his equipment. The car was the inspiration behind the Stills-Young Band's song "Long May You Run."

Young has two sons with cerebral palsy. He helped start the Bridge School for children with limited verbal abilities. Every October, artists perform at a concert to raise money for the school. Past performers include Thom Yorke of Radiohead, Metallica, Pearl Jam, and Bob Dylan. In 1985, Neil Young, Willie Nelson, and John Mellencamp founded Farm Aid, a charity that raises money for struggling family farms.

He likes to sing about the moon—it appears in at least 30 songs. He also loves to relax by paddle boarding. Another pastime is model trains, and he has made technical upgrades to the trains of the Lionel model railroading company, which he partially owns.

Alice Cooper

The Godfather of Shock Rock, born Vincent Damon Furnier, is the son of a preacher. He formed his first band at the age of 16 because he wanted to enter a local talent competition in Phoenix. They were originally called the Earwigs, but changed the name to the Spiders. They later changed the name again to Alice Cooper, and the performer legally changed his own name. Since the name was originally owned by the whole band, Cooper pays an annual royalty to his former band members.

Cooper has a Bachelor of Fine Arts. He derived his look from Bette Davis's eye makeup in *What Ever Happened to Baby Jane?* and Anita Pallenberg's outfits in *Barbarella*. Magician James Randi designed the band's stage effects, complete with a guillotine. Alice Cooper has appeared in a number of films, including Tim Burton's 2012 remake of *Dark Shadows*. In that film, the vampire Barnabas Collins refers to Cooper (he plays himself in the film) as the "ugliest woman I've ever seen."

He has also appeared on *The Muppet Show*, where he performed "Welcome to My Nightmare" and tried, like Mephistopheles in *Faust*, to trick Kermit, Gonzo, and Miss Piggy into selling their souls to the Devil. A former feud between Cooper and Marilyn Manson led to the publication of a scholarly paper in *Academic Psychiatry* called "From Alice Cooper to Marilyn Manson: The Significance of Adolescent Antiheroes."

Alice Cooper has been married to ballerina Sheryl Goddard since 1976 and claims to have been faithful to her since they've been together. As a recovered alcoholic (he stopped drinking in the '80s), he counsels other rock stars who have alcohol or drug problems. Cooper also coaches Little League baseball.

RANDOM FUN FACTS

1. Aretha Franklin taught herself to play piano by ear. She can even sing opera when the occasion requires it. She once stepped in for Pavarotti and sang "Nessun Dorma," from *Turandot*.

2. James Brown and Michael Jackson were both buried in gold-plated coffins.

3. Who is Patricia Mae Andrzejewski? Pat Benatar, of course! She enjoyed writing her memoir, *Between a Heart and a Rock Place*, so much that she decided to write a novel about the second coming of Jesus.

4. Eric Clapton is an enthusiast of mixed martial arts (MMA).

5. Elton John, whose birth name is Reginald Dwight, owns 250,000 pairs of glasses, which he keeps in their own walk-in closet. He once gave a performance in Central Park dressed as Donald Duck, and he nearly burst out laughing at several points during his rendition of "Your Song." Go look up the video—we will wait for you!

6. Eddie Money was training to be a police officer when he realized he wanted to be a musician. Along with his wife of 29 years and their five children and eight pets, he plans to produce a reality TV show about his life.

7. There is an annual festival in Germany called Zappanale, in which different bands perform Frank Zappa's music—and only Frank Zappa's music. When the region was under East German rule, the secret police harassed a Zappa fan named Wolfhard Kutz. After the fall of the Berlin Wall, Kutz found out that the secret police believed he would use Zappa's music to influence the East German youth. He organized the first Zappanale festival in 1990.

8. Peter Frampton likes a bit of trivia himself. He answered five questions correctly on *No Apparent Reason*, a trivia game on a Los Angeles radio station, becoming the all-time celebrity champion. The honor was short lived, however, as Luke Perry answered six questions just two weeks later.

9. Ozzy Osbourne was prepared for his bloody onstage antics. He used to work at a slaughterhouse!

10. Gordon Sumner, more commonly known as Sting, played Baron Harkonnen's golden-boy nephew, Feyd-Rautha, in *Dune*. The winged briefs he's wearing after his steam bath were a last-minute improvisation, as he was supposed to appear nude.

11. Jon Bon Jovi loves football and is the majority owner of the Philadelphia Soul football team.

12. Rod Stewart once wanted to become a professional football (soccer) player. He comes from a football-loving family.

13. When William Michael Albert Broad was in school, the teacher sent his parents a note that said, "Billy is idle." When he became a professional musician, he changed the spelling and took "Billy Idol" as his stage name.

14. Billy Idol and Billy Joel have more in common than their first name. Both were involved in serious motorcycle accidents. Billy Idol nearly lost his leg and Billy Joel injured both hands.

15. Iggy Pop appeared as himself in an episode of the horror TV series *Tales from the Crypt*. In that episode, a man who organized a concert for charity, in which Iggy performs, ends up killing his banker with a guitar.

16. Have you ever seen Johnny Cash perform in a color other than black? The answer is no. He always wore black onstage.

17. Elvis Costello once sang in a lemonade commercial with his father.

18. Blind since the age of seven from glaucoma, soul pianist Ray Charles had three "no's": no dog, no cane, and no guitar!

19. Politicians seem to like Tom Petty's music (Who doesn't?). He's sent cease-and-desist letters to two of them for playing his songs at their events without his consent: Michelle Bachmann for "American Girl" and George W. Bush for "I Won't Back Down."

20. Though relatively unknown in the U.S., Kate Bush is a big deal across the pond. She and novelist Emily Brontë share a birthday, and Bush's first single was "Wuthering Heights," after the novel by that author.

TEST YOURSELF – QUESTIONS AND ANSWERS

1. Which sport helped Alice Cooper recover from his alcoholism? He still plays today.

    A) Hockey

    B) Baseball

    C) Golf

2. Which city is Elvis Presley's home town?

    A) Memphis, Tennessee

    B) Tupelo, Mississippi

    C) Nashville, Tennessee

3. In which movie did Billy Idol (as himself) help the leading man win the leading lady?

    A) The Wedding Singer

    B) Love, Actually

    C) Happy Gilmore

4. The fictional rock star in *Brian Pern: A Life in Rock* is based on which real-life British rocker?

    A) Peter Gabriel

    B) Phil Collins

    C) Sting

5. Why did Roy Orbison wear sunglasses to perform?

   A) He once forgot his regular glasses on the plane.

   B) He had a condition that made him photosensitive.

   C) He didn't like the way his eyes looked.

ANSWERS

1. C
2. B
3. A
4. A
5. A

CHAPTER THREE

THE BANDS

The legendary bands are what made rock and roll what it is today. Where would rock be without the Beatles, Led Zeppelin, and the Beach Boys? With more musicians comes more drama, and many great bands broke up because of infighting, but they still left their mark on rock music. Learn more about these larger-than-life rock groups!

The Beach Boys

The California surfer boys themselves, right? Not exactly. The California part is true, but only one member, Dennis Wilson, was a surfer. They named themselves the "Pendletones," but the record label changed the name to the "Beach Boys" without consulting the young band. Brian Wilson briefly led another band on the side called Kenny & the Cadets. The Wilson brothers' mom, Audree, was one of the singers.

"I Get Around" features modulation (key change), a technique common in classical music but uncommon in pop and rock. *Pet Sounds* was one of the most innovative records in rock music history. In the songs on that record, you can hear accordions, harpsichord, vibraphone, sleigh and bicycle bells, dogs barking, silverware, and plastic water jugs, along with the usual instruments. But did you know that one of the lyricists also wrote jingles for brands such as Mattel, Gallo Wines, and Max Factor?

Remember the goats on the cover of *Pet Sounds*? Evidently, the Beach Boys weren't fond of them. The goats pushed, jumped on, and bit the band members and, according to bassist Bruce Johnston, ate a radio. And if you think the title track sounds like a James Bond theme, well, that was the intention.

The Beatles

There is little that is not known about the fab four (or five?), but perhaps you didn't know that they once bought five Greek islands with the intention of starting a utopian community. The whim didn't last long. Even rock stars mishear song lyrics—Bob Dylan thought the line "I can't hide" in "I Want To Hold Your Hand" was "I get high!" And if, like most of us, you dislike your own voice, you can take comfort in the fact that the great John Lennon felt the same way about his voice.

George Harrison loved a British candy called jelly babies. Unfortunately, fans took it a bit too far and started chucking them at him during concerts. American fans threw jelly beans, which are harder than jelly babies and, thus, painful when they hit. You probably know that Ringo was the shortest Beatle; he was 5'8" while the other three were 5'11".

"I Am the Walrus" was banned by the BBC for the word "knickers." Others were banned for real or alleged drug references. There is a street called "Penny Lane" in Liverpool. After the song was released, people started stealing the signs so often that the city stopped putting them up. They now paint the street name on the buildings.

The Beatles had a number of successful movies, but they didn't make all the ones they wanted—the fab four wanted to do "Lord of the Rings" with Stanley Kubrick. Both Tolkien and Kubrick opposed the idea, so it never panned out. They even knew which parts they wanted to play: George would have been Gandalf because, of course he would; who else? A less obvious casting call was John as Gollum, but that's the role he wanted. Paul wanted to be Frodo and Ringo wanted to be Sam. That's not hard to visualize, actually. *The Jungle Book* director, Wolfgang Reitherman, really wanted the Beatles to do the voice acting for the vultures, but John decided that wasn't a good fit.

The Rolling Stones

The bad boys of rock may have been the first to use the word "groupie." Their history goes back further than the band: Keith Richards and Mick Jagger have known each other since they were five years old. Both were already interested in music. Mick Jagger's distinctive voice is partially due to the fact that he accidentally bit off part of his tongue as a child. Even with Jagger's famous mouth, the Stones claim that their "tongue" logo comes from the Hindu goddess Kali.

"Satisfaction" was almost a very different song. Hard to imagine, but it was originally played on a harmonica. The Stones also had to sing "Let's Spend Some Time Together," instead of "Let's Spend the Night Together," to appear on *The Ed Sullivan Show*. Some people like their songs just the way they are though, such as Martin Scorsese. His song of choice is "Gimme Shelter," and he has used it in four movies.

The Rolling Stones like to play snooker, and they always have a table for it when touring. Keith Richards loves shepherd's pie, and he has to have it when on tour. And he has to be the one to break the crust (people have been fired for digging in before him). The rest of the band members like pie, too. They started a custard pie fight in a roomful of journalists at their launch of *Beggars Banquet*.

The Monkees

The Monkees were created for TV and their music was tightly controlled by their managers at the beginning, so the pre-fab four had very little input as to what they performed. The show's casting call invited "4 insane boys" to try out, and further specified "spirited Ben Frank's-types." The latter requirement referred to the types of guys who hung out at a coffee shop on Sunset Strip.

The show was supposed to depict a band that was an

unsuccessful Beatles imitation, but the group ended up becoming one of the best bands of the '60s. By the way, did you know that the full version of Peter Tork's surname is Thorkelson? Also, talent often runs in families—Mike Nesmith's mom, Bette Nesmith Graham, invented Liquid Paper in 1956.

Botched your last job interview? Don't worry, Mike Nesmith showed up to the audition holding his laundry bag, and he still got the job. They got along well with the Beatles, and John Lennon called them "the Marx Brothers of rock." The Monkees had their own imitators—*Star Trek*'s Pavel Chekov was based on Davy Jones, and it was a ploy to get more teens (especially girls) to watch the series!

The Who

Guitarist Pete Townshend was the storyteller of the group. He was the one who came up with the stories that became the double albums (and rock operas) *Tommy* and *Quadrophenia*. He's known for his stage technique of swinging his arm around like a windmill while strumming his guitar. This move most likely inspired rock fans to play "air guitar." He later admitted he'd copied the move after seeing Keith Richards do it once. Richards himself seemed to think the technique was silly and not worth repeating.

If Townshend was the storyteller, then drummer Keith Moon was the troublemaker. His birthday party ended with a car in the hotel swimming pool, resulting in the band being barred from Holiday Inn (yes, all Holiday Inns). Due to his substance abuse issues, he once passed out during a concert. An amateur drummer from the audience took his place for the concert, and it went surprisingly well.

The Who has had a few different drummers. Their present drummer is Zak Starkey—Ringo Starr's son! The filming of *Tommy* was quite eventful. Ann-Margret had to have stitches in her hand after cutting it on a broken TV. Do you remember the scene where a building in Tommy's holiday camp burned down? Well, it was an accidental fire (but on a pier in Southsea, not the building), and the fire crews were real.

Strawberry Alarm Clock

There are a lot of strange band names out there, and this is certainly one of them. The band members were fans of the Beatles and their song "Strawberry Fields Forever," and they wanted to use "strawberry" in their own name. Then someone noticed an old alarm clock in the room, and "Strawberry Alarm Clock" was christened. In 2012, the reunited band produced their first studio album since 1969, called "Wake Up Where You Are."

They're often referred to as a "one-hit wonder" because "Incense and Peppermints" is the only song many are familiar with. Did you know that the lead vocals in that song were not sung by a band member? A 16-year-old friend of the band, Greg Mumford, happened to be in the studio when they were recording the song, and he sang for the demo recording. The plan was to add the other band member's voice later, but the producers preferred Mumford's rendition.

Ever the psychedelic band, they were fond of caftans and magic carpets. They used to sit on the carpets and allow their roadies to carry them to the stage. Strawberry Alarm Clock also made two movies, in which they appear as themselves: *Beyond the Valley of the Dolls* and *Psych-Out*. The latter film was mostly written by Jack Nicholson, and he played the leading role. The band played "Incense and Peppermints" in both films, and that song appears on the soundtracks of various other movies, including Austin Powers: International Man of Mystery.

The Kinks

Originally called the Ravens and the Bo Weevils, the Kinks were founded by brothers Ray and Dave Davies. The two boys, who had six older sisters, attended the same London school as Rod Stewart. When they decided to form a band, Stewart was briefly the lead singer. He left the band in 1962 to form his own, the Moonrakers, and the two bands were rivals.

Unfortunately, the band members did not get along well, as seen in a fight that broke out between Dave Davies and drummer Mick Avory onstage during a concert. Avory walloped

Davies over the head with his hi-hat stand, and Davies needed 16 stitches. To avoid being arrested, the band had to pretend the fight was part of an experimental onstage act. Such antics may have been the reason they were banned from touring in the U.S. at first.

They still achieved fame, though, with "You Really Got Me." Fans loved the guitar riff. To get that loud, distorted sound, Dave Davies made a slice in his amp speaker. Like many artists in the '60s, Ray Davies was fascinated by Indian music and culture and incorporated some Eastern elements in his music. His most notable result was "See My Friends." The inspiration for the song came from Davies's visit to Bombay, where he heard local fishermen chanting in the morning.

Pink Floyd

Three of the founding members of Pink Floyd met in university, where they were all studying architecture. The band's name changed several times: Sigma 6, the Meggadeaths, the Abdabs, Leonard's Lodgers, and the Tea Set. Finally, guitarist Syd Barrett named the band after two blues musicians—Pink Anderson and Floyd Council.

One of the most successful bands in history, their 1973 album *The Dark Side of the Moon* remained on the Billboard Top 200 for nearly 16 years! Did you hear the rumor that it synchronizes exactly with *The Wizard of Oz*? Well, it doesn't, but drummer

Nick Mason deadpanned that they'd intended it to match *The Sound of Music* instead.

Pink Floyd was known for their multimedia performances. They used a film projector starting in 1966. Later, they graduated to inflatable flying pigs, pyrotechnics, and live surround sound— which they were the first to use. Sometimes, these innovations didn't go over so well. They were banned from several venues because of the pyrotechnics, and the pig once floated away and got into Heathrow's flight path.

Speaking of animals, have you seen the album cover for their album *Animals*? It features a flying pig behind the Battersea Power Station. The name, the cover, and much of the lyrical content on the album were inspired by George Orwell's *Animal Farm*. Another album cover, for *Wish You Were Here*, shows a businessman who is on fire. The fire was real and the businessman was a stunt man. Despite the safety precautions, he ended up with a singed mustache.

The list of Pink Floyd's accomplishments is almost endless. One claim to fame is that they were the first rock band to be played in space. Russian Cosmonauts took *Delicate Sound of Thunder* with them to the MIR space station in 1989. And speaking of space, Douglas Adams, author of *Hitchhiker's Guide to the Galaxy*, named their album *The Division Bell*.

The Grateful Dead

The Grateful Dead and the Velvet Underground have something in common—they were both once known as the Warlocks. Jerry Garcia, who studied at the Art Institute in San Francisco, came up with the name "Grateful Dead" while reading a folklore dictionary. Before Garcia became a musician, he picked beans and apricots in the fields.

Jerry Garcia was known for his guitar playing, but did you know that his first instrument was a banjo? And Phil Lesh only started playing bass when he joined the band—he was a classically trained trumpeter. The Grateful Dead saw themselves as an egalitarian band and composed several songs together. The group compositions were credited to "McGannahan Skjellyfetti."

The Grateful Dead inspired fans beyond the music, even in the business world. At least two business books have been inspired by the band: *Marketing Lessons from the Grateful Dead: What Every Business Can Learn from the Most Iconic Band in History* and *Everything I Know About Business I Learned from the Grateful Dead: The Ten Most Innovative Lessons from a Long, Strange Trip*.

Have you seen the '80s remake of *The Twilight Zone*? The Grateful Dead wrote the music for the opening and closing credits. You (or your parents) may have had a Jerry Garcia tie or a Grateful Dead shirt. However, some say the "dancing" bears are supposed to look like they're marching.

Jefferson Airplane

The face of psychedelic hedonism was made famous by the contralto, vibrato vocals of Grace Slick, who was a former model. She was the one who wrote their most famous songs, "Somebody to Love" and "White Rabbit." Slick was born in the year of the rabbit and, when she was a child, lived next door to a man who had 40 white rabbits (most likely for fur coats). She now keeps rabbits as pets and feeds raccoons.

"White Rabbit" was, however, mostly inspired by *Alice's Adventures in Wonderland*, which Grace Slick's parents used to read to her. She says that the rabbit represents curiosity, and Alice follows him. Slick also wrote the song to point out the hypocrisy of adults that promote such literature and wonder why their kids grow up to take drugs. Before writing the song, Slick listened to *Sketches of Spain* by Miles Davis for a full day.

"White Rabbit" and "Somebody to Love" appear on *Surrealistic Pillow*. Jerry Garcia was the one to suggest the name, saying the music on it was "as surrealistic as a pillow is soft." He is credited on the album as the band's "spiritual adviser." After leaving the band, Slick became the first known rock star to attend Alcoholics Anonymous, and she exhibits her own paintings.

Led Zeppelin

The members of Led Zeppelin were aficionados of Tolkien, Celtic mythology, and folklore They are often cited as the first real metal band. Despite the band's technological abilities in the recording studio, you can hear phones ringing and John Bonham's squeaky drum pedals in the background of some of their songs, such as "The Ocean," "The Rain Song," and "Dancing Days."

Not everyone was a Led Zeppelin fan. Countess Frau Eva von Zeppelin called the band "shrieking monkeys" and threatened to sue them for using her family's name. To avoid this, they called themselves "The Nobs" when touring Copenhagen. The band didn't limit their inspiration to Middle Earth and ancient Britain. However, "Kashmir" is not about the region of Kashmir. The song was inspired by Robert Plant's time in Morocco. There's also "Going to California." This one was about Joni Mitchell, who Robert Plant was infatuated with.

Blue Öyster Cult

The band once known as Soft White Underbelly has been called the "American Black Sabbath and "the world's brainiest heavy metal band." Lead singer (though they always took turns singing lead) Eric Bloom once said they were among the shortest bands in rock. Lead guitarist Buck Dharma was only 5'2" and Bloom was 5'7". However, there were shorter bands, such as the Small Faces.

Speaking of Buck Dharma, he was entirely self-taught on guitar. Blue Öyster Cult is known for its cabalistic lyrics, but they're mostly influenced by the band's interested in sci-fi and fantasy. Aside from Patti Smith, the group had a journalist and a fantasy author contribute to their lyrics. They also had authors as fans, such as Stephen King and J.K. Rowling. Under her pseudonym Robert Galbraith, Rowling incorporated several Blue Öyster Cult songs into her latest detective novel, *Career of Evil*. The band members themselves were bookworms, as noted by a surprised reporter who went to their dressing room for an interview and found them all sitting around reading instead of partying.

Eric Bloom was the band's acoustic engineer before he was their lead singer. He likes martial arts and *Star Trek* (the term "stun guitar" comes from *Star Trek*), and on at least one occasion brought his lunch to the studio in a KORG lunch box. To get Eric Bloom's onstage "biker" look, manager Sandy Pearlman took him to a "gay store" to buy black leather. Bloom said the outfit made him feel like Batman.

They were also one of the first bands to use lasers in their concerts. Scientists even came to their concerts to take notes. The band eventually stopped using the lasers because they were expensive. Oh, and what happened to the band's first lead singer? Jeff Kagel left the band early on, went to India, and became Krishna Das. He sings a spiritual music called "kirtan" and was called the "Pavarotti of kirtan" by *Yoga Journal*.

Rush

Rush is the definitive progressive rock band, with all three band members virtuosos on their instruments. Known for his ability to hit high notes, bassist and lead singer Geddy Lee has a three-octave range. When he's not playing music, Lee likes to watch and read about baseball. He participates in the games, too. He inaugurated the Toronto Blue Jays' 2013 season by throwing the first pitch, and he sang the Canadian national anthem for the 1993 Major League Baseball All-Star Game.

Drummer Neil Peart wrote most of the band's lyrics, drawing on literature, mythology, philosophy, and sci-fi, among other topics. And lyrics aren't all he writes: he's written several nonfiction books, most of them about his extensive travels. He also has a racing team called "Bangers N' Mash." Known for his intricate drum solos, Peart once called playing drums with Rush "running a marathon while solving equations." Early in his career, he started playing drums with the base of his sticks instead of the tips. Initially, this was to save money, as the tips would break off and he'd have to replace the sticks, but then he got used to the bigger sound.

Unlike most other rock bands, Rush doesn't use amplifier stacks, so they fill the space with house appliances such as a fully-stocked fridge, working dryers full of custom-made Rush t-shirts (given to the audience after the concert), and rotisserie chicken ovens that were tended by a "chef"—and all of these appliances were miked!

Queen

Legendary singer Freddie Mercury's voice was so unusual that it's been the subject of scientific studies, with the conclusion that his vocal cords moved abnormally fast and he used a technique called subharmonics, used by Tuvan throat singers. Pretty impressive, especially since he did it all with no formal voice training!

Freddie Mercury's stage antics included performing on Darth Vader's shoulder's and Superman's back. Like John Lennon, he was a cat person, with over ten cats at one time. He often phoned them when he was traveling. Mercury nearly collaborated with Michael Jackson on an album, but objected to the presence of Jackson's llama in the studio. He was friends with Princess Diana. One night, she asked Mercury to take her to a gay bar, and he dressed her as a (very handsome) man. Her presence was undetected, as everyone was focused on Freddie.

Though Mercury is the most famous member of Queen, guitarist Brian May should not be overlooked. When he was a teenager, he made a guitar from scratch (from his home's mantelpiece), and this is the guitar he used in concerts for 30 years. He has a PhD in astrophysics and applied his knowledge in physics in the studio to achieve different sounds when recording. He and astronaut Rusty Schweickart are co-founders of the educational campaign "Asteroid Day." Speaking of space, Mercury incorporated all four band members' zodiac signs into Queen's logo.

Kiss

The band once known as "Wicked Lester" is not only one of the most-recognized rock bands in the world; they also have a line of "Kiss Kaskets." Dimebag Darrell, guitarist of Pantera, was buried in one. The band had also planned to produce a line of jeans, but it didn't work out.

Most of the band members perform under names they weren't born with. Vocalist and bassist Gene Simmons's real name is Chaim Witz, and he once wanted to become a Rabbi. Guitarist Paul Stanley, in contrast, majored in art. A lot of art goes into the musicians' onstage look, with the wild outfits and full makeup, and it hasn't always gone on smoothly. Ace Frehley developed an allergy to the silver makeup that was part of his look, and had to switch to blue eyeshadow. He also once spray painted his hair silver, thinking it would wash out. It didn't.

Despite the band's wild image and notorious backstage shenanigans, they did not curse onstage in the years they performed in makeup, since their look at that time attracted younger fans. Speaking of young people, in "God of Thunder," you can hear children's voices in the background. They are the producer's sons.

Metallica

James Hetfield doesn't understand Metallica co-founder Lars Ulrich's love of pancakes. The drummer says he eats up to 20 pancakes per day, made of oats, yogurt, egg whites, and Stevia, insisting it's one key to his good health. One of Hetfield's hobbies is beekeeping. Guitarist Kirk Hammett replaced Dave Mustaine, but he almost didn't audition because he thought the invitation was a prank.

While thrash metal is not known for connections to literature, Metallica is not just any band. Their most obvious literary song is "For Whom the Bell Tolls," but the band members (particularly late bassist Cliff Burton) were also fans of classic horror writer H.P. Lovecraft. "The Thing that Should Not Be" and "The Call of Ktulu" were inspired by Lovecraft's Cthulhu mythos. And if you're thinking, "They misspelled Cthulhu," well, of course they did! Writing the Old One's name correctly can summon him. You might want to look behind you...

Does the opening riff to "Don't Tread On Me" sound familiar? It's taken from "America" in *West Side Story*. If you think you've heard Metallica band members' voices in cartoons, you may be right. Ulrich and Hetfield voiced two dragons on the Disney series *Dave the Barbarian*, and Hetfield sang "Hell Isn't Good" in *South Park: Bigger, Longer & Uncut*.

U2

All four band members met in high school. Paul David Hewson, a.k.a. Bono, also met his future wife at the same school. His nickname comes from "Bono vox," which was a local hearing aid company and also means "good voice" in Latin. David Howell Evans got the nickname "the Edge" for his angular features. The band was originally called Feedback, possibly because they took a while to produce good sound.

U2 has produced 14 studio albums to date, the first being *Boy*. The cover features the young nephew of a friend, and the boy also appeared on the cover of *War*, three years later. From *Joshua Tree*, "One Tree Hill" is about a roadie and friend of the band who died in a motorcycle accident in 1986. The vocals you hear in the song are Bono's first take. He couldn't bring himself to sing it more than once.

The bands that have opened for U2 include the Dalton Brothers, a country group. In an Indianapolis show, they sang a Hank Williams song and an original ballad. The fans nearest the stage eventually realized that the country band was U2 in disguise.

RANDOM FUN FACTS

1. The music of the Zombies took a bit longer to catch on than that of other British Invasion bands. By the time "Time of the Season" became a serious hit, the band had broken up!

2. The Mamas & the Papas got their name when Cass Elliot—who did *not* choke on a ham sandwich—found out that the Hells Angels called female bikers "mamas." So she and Michelle became "mamas" and the guys became "papas."

3. Sly and the Family Stone was one of the first racially integrated bands. While multi-instrumentalist Sly and most of the band are black, drummer Greg Errico and saxophonist Jerry Martini are white. Also, in an era where it was uncommon for women to play instruments onstage, Cynthia Robinson and Rosie Stone did: trumpet and keyboards.

4. Singer and flautist Ian Anderson, of progressive rock band Jethro Tull, owned a salmon farm for many years. He is also father-in-law to Andrew Lincoln, the lead character on *The Walking Dead*.

5. Black Sabbath went through a few names before choosing the one we all know, and one of them was "Blues Band Margarine." When Ozzy left the band, several singers

auditioned to take his place, including Michael Bolotin. Sound familiar? Michael Bolton!

6. Texan band ZZ Top is recognizable for their long, full beards. Except for the drummer, who doesn't have a long beard, and his name is... Frank Beard.

7. Hardcore Deep Purple fans might know that hard-rocking guitarist Ritchie Blackmore, not only went on to form half of the folk/rock duo Blackmore's Night, but he also has around 2,000 albums of Renaissance music.

8. It was the Canadian-American band Steppenwolf who unintentionally gave a name to the harder rock sounds that had emerged in the mid to late '60s. The phrase "heavy metal" in "Born to Be Wild" refers to a motorcycle, but was quickly adopted into the rock music vocabulary.

9. "Take It To The Limit," one of the Eagles' hit songs, was sung by bassist Randy Meisner. He was the only one who could hit the high notes—but that was in the studio. Onstage, he would get nervous and have trouble with the notes. Unfortunately for him, the song was a fan favorite and the rest of the band insisted that he sing it. This was a factor in Meisner's decision to leave the band.

10. Most people know about Van Halen's infamous no–brown-M&Ms clause, but is it really just a "crazy celebrity" thing? No. The M&Ms line is strategically located in the middle of

their long, detailed concert contract, which gives the organizers crucial information about the band's heavy, expensive equipment and how it should be set up. If the band members find brown M&Ms, they know the concert organizers did not read the contract properly, and they need to check the setup for potentially dangerous problems.

11. It wasn't easy for female rockers in the male-dominated music industry. Ann and Nancy Wilson were the leaders of American-Canadian band Heart, and they wrote all the band's music and played instruments onstage. All this combined to make the sisters pioneers in the rock world.

12. Hundreds of rumors have circulated about Fleetwood Mac throughout their long career. One rumor is that singer Stevie Nicks is a witch. It seems to have sprung from her song "Rhiannon" (Mick Fleetwood described her performance of that song as "an exorcism on stage") and her flowing black clothes. To quell the rumors, she stopped wearing black onstage for some time.

13. When Scorpions visited France, they were informed that there had been a baby boom nine months after the peak popularity of "Still Loving You."

14. When English band Def Leppard advertised for a new drummer in 1978, Rick Allen was only 14 years old, and his mom answered the ad for him. He lost his left arm in a car

accident in 1984 and learned to play with a custom drum set that uses foot pedals to do what his arm used to do.

15. Former Guns N' Roses guitarist Saul Hudson, better known as Slash, is a dinosaur enthusiast and collects dinosaur art. Most people know about his snakes, but he's also donated money to zoos, especially to keep the L.A. Zoo's Pachyderm Forest from closing.

16. How did Foreigner get their name? Well, three of the band's members were American and the other three were British, so they were foreigners wherever they went.

17. The Animals were supposed to tour Japan at one point, but the trip was cut short when their manager was kidnapped by the yakuza. He was forced to sign an IOU but managed to scribble down that it was signed under duress. None of his kidnappers could read English, so they released him on the condition that they leave Japan or be killed.

18. The Doors performed on *The Ed Sullivan Show* once before being banned. They were instructed not to sing the word "higher" when performing "Light My Fire," but did so anyway.

19. The band Chicago was once known as The Big Thing. Known now for love songs, they used to sing political material protesting Richard Nixon, air pollution, and the military industrial complex.

20. Though Nirvana and Pearl Jam achieved commercial success first, Soundgarden was the first Seattle grunge band to be signed by a major label. In Sand Point Park in Seattle, there is a sculpture made of pipes, through which the wind blows and makes noise. The sculpture is called "A Sound Garden," hence, the band's name.

TEST YOURSELF – QUESTIONS AND ANSWERS

1. Which '60s band featured three of the greatest rock guitarists, one by one: Eric Clapton, Jimmy Page, and Jeff Beck?

    A) Cream

    B) The Yardbirds

    C) Led Zeppelin

2. The Eagles first formed as a backup band for which singer?

    A) Joan Baez

    B) Don Henley

    C) Linda Ronstadt

3. Which band did VH1 decide not to feature on *Behind the Music* because their lives were not interesting enough?

    A) Kansas

    B) Duran Duran

    C) Foreigner

4. Lynyrd Skynyrd had to stop playing one of their songs because fans were throwing what onto the stage?

    A) Bullets

    B) Birds

    C) Tomatoes

5. In 1996, alternative band Nerf Herder annoyed this classic rock band by writing a song about them, complaining that their music had gone downhill:

A) Aerosmith

B) Van Halen

C) Metallica

ANSWERS

1. B
2. C
3. A
4. A
5. B

CHAPTER FOUR
THE HITS

How did the guitarist come up with that epic riff and what does "Crimson and Clover" mean? Was "Peggy Sue" Buddy Holly's girlfriend and what on earth is "Smells Like Teen Spirit" about? All songs have stories behind them, and some are tragic, bizarre, or absolutely hilarious. Find out some of the most interesting stories here!

Peggy Sue

In 1957, Buddy Holly wrote a song for his baby niece, Cindy Lou. However, the Crickets' drummer, Jerry Allison, had recently broken up with his girlfriend, Peggy Sue. Allison wanted to get back together with Peggy Sue, and he convinced Buddy Holly to name the song after her. It worked, and the couple reunited and later married. They divorced in 1967.

Fast-forward to 2008: Peggy Sue Gerron published her memoir, *Whatever Happened to Peggy Sue*, in which she claims that the song was always about her, and that the late singer had proposed that they should divorce their respective spouses and he would "take care of" her. The book gave Buddy Holly's widow, who is not well-liked by some of Holly's family and fans, a world of vexation and provided a feast for the gossip mills, but the author's claims do not appear to be based on fact. I guess we'll never know...

Good Vibrations

Ranking sixth on *Rolling Stone*'s 500 Greatest Songs of All Time, between "Respect" by Aretha Franklin and "Johnny B. Goode" by Chuck Berry, "Good Vibrations" is an incredibly complex rock song that was years ahead of its time. Brian Wilson, the musical genius and brains behind the Beach Boys, called the song a "pocket symphony."

What's that unusual, high-pitched instrument playing in the hook and at the end? It's an electro-theremin, or simply, "the box." Named after its Soviet inventor, the traditional theremin is an electric instrument with metal antennas, which you play by moving your hands around the antennas. It's extremely difficult. Inventor and trombonist Paul Tanner had recently developed a similar-sounding instrument without antennas, which was easier to manage, and he played it for the recording. Since they couldn't drag Paul Tanner along on tour and the song was often requested, they had to modify a synthesizer to get a similar sound for concerts.

The fast rhythm in the background is made by a cello, which is not normally thought of as a "rhythm" instrument. Brian Wilson wanted sessions keyboardist Don Randi to play a drawn-out tone by holding down the bass pedal of the organ. Randi finally got the sound Wilson wanted when he took a pillow and fell asleep with his head on the pedal. While the lyrics are about a connection with a "flower-power" hippie girl, the phrase "good vibrations" was inspired by the Wilson brothers' mom, Audree. When Brian was 14, she told him that dogs can sense the vibrations of different humans, and that's why they bark at certain people and not others.

Yellow Submarine

Barbiturates, right? At least that's what your grumpy uncle told you. Actually, no. The nickname for the drugs came shortly after the song. Like "Puff the Magic Dragon" by Peter, Paul and Mary, it is a simple story for children. Paul envisioned a yellow submarine as a children's toy and made up a story about an old sailor talking about his voyages and his yellow submarine.

Paul kept the melody simple since he was writing it for Ringo— the drummer's vocal range was a bit narrower than that of the others, and he sang better in non-serious songs. They had a lot of fun in the studio with the sound effects. John used a straw to blow bubbles into a bucket of water, and an employee swirled chains around in a full bathtub. A roadie walked around the studio playing a big bass drum as a bunch of the band's friends, including Marianne Faithfull, Mick Jagger, Pattie (Boyd) Harrison, and Brian Jones, sang with them for the chorus.

Scottish singer Donovan helped Paul with the line "Sky of blue, sea of green." Paul returned the favor by playing bass on Donovan's song "Mellow Yellow" and joining in the cheering at the end. Like "Yellow Submarine," "Mellow Yellow" was thought to be about drugs, but wasn't. It was, however, partially about a ladies' yellow vibrator on the market that looked like a banana.

A Day in the Life

Of course, the Beatles had lots of interesting songs. This song begins with the words, "I read the news today," and it really was about several items in the news at that time. The first was the death of Tara Browne, a friend of the band and the heir to the Guinness fortune. The details of his death in the song are fictional. The "4,000 holes" refer to potholes, and the "turn you on" line has a double meaning.

The instrumental components are complex and they were not easy to play. The members of a 41-piece orchestra in party hats were instructed to play their instruments louder and louder into a glissando, each as individuals without listening to the rest of the orchestra. This was not what they were used to. To play the final chord, assistant Mal Evans, John, and Ringo each sat at a piano. They had to strike E major at the exact same time, and nine takes were required to get it right. Not all of it was hard, though. The alarm clock was easy enough, though it was intended as a joke and not intended to be in there!

Johnny B. Goode

Rock songs about rock stars, such as "Turn the Page" by Bob Seger and "Shooting Star" by Bad Company, are staples of the rock canon, but Chuck Berry wrote the first one. "Johnny B. Goode" is autobiographical, but loosely so—Berry, unlike "Johnny," was well educated and came from St. Louis, not New Orleans. The "country boy" line was originally "colored boy," but Berry knew that line wouldn't be played on white radio stations.

The name was a combination of the street he grew up on (Goode) and piano player Johnnie Johnson, who collaborated with Berry, as well as with Keith Richards and Eric Clapton. Incidentally, Johnson released a solo album in 1991 called *Johnnie B. Bad*. Many earlier country and blues musicians did not sing their words clearly, but Berry did, so that listeners could understand his carefully crafted story. It worked, because the song was launched into space in 1977 aboard Voyager I. It was part of a compilation of the best of American culture.

As Tears Go By

Mick Jagger and Keith Richards wrote "As Tears Go By" when the Rolling Stones' manager locked them in the kitchen and forbade them to come out until they'd written a song that wasn't about sex. They wrote "As Tears Go By" and, because the Stones didn't do ballads at the time, gave the song to Marianne Faithfull, and she made it a hit. The Stones also recorded it the following year with only strings, voice, and acoustic guitar.

If you've ever scratched your head and wondered what it means for tears to go by, you're not alone. In fact, the original title was "As Time Goes By," but that was also a song from *Casablanca*, so they changed it. The theme of the song—nostalgia that one's childhood is over—seemed a rather odd one for 17-year-old Faithfull and 22-year-old Jagger to sing. Faithfull re-recorded the song in 1987 and was able to capture the tone of the lyrics much better.

Crimson and Clover

There are a lot of opinions out there about this one by Tommy James and the Shondells, usually involving sex or drugs. If that's what you're expecting, Tommy James's account may be a bit of a letdown. Two words that he liked just came to him as he was getting out of bed one morning, and they sounded nice together. James then filled in the rest of the song with the band's drummer, Pete Lucia. It was the first song they wrote after their outside writer quit, and it remained on the *Billboard* Hot 100 chart for 16 weeks.

Lucia's account differs slightly. He claims the idea came to him while he was watching a football game in which one team was wearing red jerseys and the other green. The song has been covered by many other artists, most successfully by Joan Jett in 1982. Prince also did a cover that combined this song with "Wild Thing."

Layla

Layla and Other Assorted Love Songs was the only studio album by Derek and the Dominos, led by Eric Clapton. At least three of the love songs on the album were about model Pattie Boyd, with whom Clapton had fallen in love, and who happened to be George Harrison's wife at the time. Years later, Boyd would divorce Harrison and marry Clapton, with Harrison's blessing.

Clapton took the name of the song from a story of unrequited love that originated in Arabia and was expanded upon by Persian poets, particularly Nizami. In some versions of the story, Layla is a princess, and in others, she is a slave (as is Majnun). In every version of the story, Majnun is not allowed to marry Layla, and his love drives him mad and he composes copious amounts of poetry.

"Layla" lasts over seven minutes, which was too long for a single at that time. The end features a long piano solo that doesn't sound like it belongs with the song. That's because it wasn't written for this song—drummer Jim Gordon added it, but he had taken it from his former girlfriend, Rita Coolidge. Also near the end is an electric guitar flourish that sounds like a bird. This was intended by Duane Allman as a tribute to Charlie "Bird" Parker. A French artist, Frandsen De Schonberg, painted the cover art, which features a blonde woman who resembles Pattie Boyd.

The songs on *Layla and Other Assorted Love Songs* aren't the only ones Eric Clapton wrote for Boyd. "Wonderful Tonight" was written during their marriage, on an evening she took a long time to get ready, and he wrote "Old Love" at the end of their relationship.

Sympathy for the Devil

Marianne Faithfull gave Mick Jagger a book called *The Master and Margarita* by Soviet/Russian author Mikhail Bulgakov, in which the Devil and his cronies spend half a week playing pranks, with quite serious consequences, on the citizens of 1930s Moscow. The book is considered one of the best Soviet satires. Along with Baudelaire, it was the inspiration for the Rolling Stones' 1968 song "Sympathy for the Devil."

As you can imagine (or remember), this song generated an incredible amount of controversy. Despite the band's insistence that the song illustrates man's dark side and does not celebrate Satanism—the historical atrocities in the song were done by humans, after all. There was also a rumor that the stabbing at the Altamont festival took place during this song, but the band was actually playing "Under My Thumb" at the time. Still, the Stones didn't perform "Sympathy for the Devil" in concert for seven years.

The song was written as a folk tune with acoustic instruments and was reinvented in the studio several times until the band decided on a samba rhythm. You can hear a cowbell and congas in the song.

Like a Rolling Stone

No, this is not about the rock group or the magazine. Bob Dylan took it from the proverb "a rolling stone gathers no moss." It was 1965, and Dylan was tired and bored of the music he'd been playing on tour. He wrote a short story in loose verse about a debutante who fell from high society and became an outcast and, from there, "Like a Rolling Stone" was born.

No one knows for sure if the song is about a specific woman, but a likely candidate is Edie Sedgwick, a rich girl who ran away from home, became involved with Andy Warhol's "Factory" crowd, received her "15 minutes of fame" (this expression was coined by Warhol), and was discarded. Warhol's crowd believed that the diplomat on the chrome horse referred to him. This idea is further strengthened by the fact that Dylan and Sedgwick had been romantically involved, but it is still just a theory.

The song is also remarkable for its length, at just over six minutes. At that time, radio stations rarely played anything longer than three minutes, but listeners demanded to hear Dylan's full version. Dylan's vocal style also inspired a generation of musicians, including Jimi Hendrix and Sam Cooke, by proving that you don't need a conventional voice to be a rock star. Hendrix covered this song, as well as "All Along The Watchtower."

Smoke on the Water

Everyone knows the guitar riff of this rock anthem by Deep Purple, but few know the lyrics beyond the chorus. If you listen to the lyrics, however, you'll learn the whole story behind this song, and it's a true one: the fire at a Frank Zappa concert, started by a "stupid with a flare gun," that burned the Montreux Casino to the ground. Deep Purple was in town to record at the casino and was staying at the hotel across the lake, from where they saw the fire and immediately wrote about it.

"Funky Claude" refers to Claude Nobs, the organizer of the Montreux Jazz Festival and the Frank Zappa concert. The fact that there were no serious injuries was partially because Nobs really did carry teens out of the building. Shortly after the fire, the band played the song for Nobs but said they did not plan to include it on their album. He convinced them that it would be a huge hit.

Baba O'Riley

No, this song by the Who is not called "Teenage Wasteland." Pete Townshend named the song after two people he admired: Indian spiritual guru Meher Baba and Terry Riley, a minimalist composer. Townshend imagined a song that would result from entering Meher Baba's life into a synthesizer, but the song ended up reflecting more of Terry Riley's ideas.

The Who was planning a project called *Lifehouse*, a rock opera like *Tommy.* This song was supposed to be sung by a Scottish farmer who is moving to London with his family. The "teenage wasteland" refers to Woodstock. The violin at the end was drummer Keith Moon's idea, but Roger Daltrey plays that part on harmonica in concerts.

American Pie

Most people know that Don McLean's 1971 hit is about the deaths of Buddy Holly, Ritchie Valens, and the Big Bopper. McLean also saw that event as a turning point, from the relatively innocent '50s to the more volatile '60s. The future singer was a 13-year-old paperboy at the time of the plane crash. He dedicated the album to Buddy Holly, hoping to renew interest in Holly's life and music.

McLean declined to explain the meaning of the song until 2015, when the original manuscript was auctioned. He then confirmed that "the king" was Elvis and "the jester" was Bob Dylan. "Helter skelter" is a reference to the Charles Manson murders and the fifth verse describes the Altamont Free Concert, during which a teenager was stabbed to death by a group of Hells Angels.

If you listen closely, you may notice that the song begins in mono and switches to stereo to illustrate the changes in musical style with the times. Weird Al created a Star Wars–themed parody to the song called "The Saga Begins." Don McLean (and his children) liked the parody and claimed that Weird Al's lyrics often come to mind when he (McLean) performs "American Pie." (George Lucas loved the song too.)

Godzilla

Thanks to the lyrical talent behind Blue Öyster Cult, many of their songs have interesting stories behind them, whether from sci-fi or fantasy, or a reference to popular or motorcycle culture. "Godzilla" was one of their biggest hits, along with "Don't Fear the Reaper" and "Burnin' for You," and it is pretty much a satire of the genre they were masters of. Buck Dharma played a guitar riff and, being a fan of monster movies, thought of Godzilla.

A huge, moving Godzilla monster with flashing red eyes and smoke coming out of its mouth used to share the stage with them for live performances of the song. Vocalist and stun guitarist Eric Bloom spoke some Japanese in the second half of the song. When the movie *Godzilla* was remade in 1998, the song was passed over in favor of one by P. Diddy. Bloom and Dharma recorded a parody of their own song, calling it "NoZilla," with lyrics mocking the director's decision.

Later, when the guitarist became the leader of the Buck Dharma Band, he heard about a kid who was using "Godzilla" to help him fight an inoperable brain tumor. The kid was successfully treated in an experimental process. The band went to Atlanta, where the boy was, and performed a benefit concert to cover his medical bills.

Hotel California

At some point, someone's probably told you this song by the Eagles is about a mental institution or Church of Satan. Actually, it's about the excesses in the rock and roll lifestyle in L.A. As seen in the lives (and deaths) of so many stars, these excesses are hard to avoid if you're rich and famous. In contrast with the dark thematic material, the original working title was "Mexican Reggae."

The song includes a playful reference to the group Steely Dan in the "steely knives" line. The word "colitas" refers to marijuana. Guitarist Don Felder came up with the melody while resting at a beach house in Malibu and Don Henley and Glenn Frey wrote the lyrics. Frey imagined the desert scene and a traveler who stops and finds a bunch of strange characters, like an episode of the Twilight Zone.

Silver Springs

Most people know that *Rumours* chronicles the complicated relationships between the members of Fleetwood Mac, but what about the song that didn't make it onto the album? "Silver Springs," like most of the songs on *Rumours*, is a breakup song. Stevie Nicks wrote it at the end of her relationship with Lindsey Buckingham to describe what could have been. As for the title, Stevie Nicks noticed the road sign when they were driving through Silver Spring, Maryland and thought it sounded like a romantic name for a beautiful place.

Nicks badly wanted "Silver Springs" on *Rumours*, especially since Buckingham's breakup song to her, "Go Your Own Way," was particularly scathing (the song accuses her of "shacking up," which was untrue, and Nicks said she wanted to kill him every time they performed that song). Mick Fleetwood and the others took "Silver Springs" off the album for various reasons, including its length and the fact that there were enough slow songs. The song finally appeared on *The Chain* in 1992 (a boxed set) and on their greatest hits album.

Born in the U.S.A.

Sounds patriotic, right? Not if you listen beyond the chorus—which then-President Ronald Reagan obviously failed to do, as he used "Born in the U.S.A." as his campaign song and praised Bruce Springsteen for promoting the American dream (Reagan's opponent Walter Mondale mentioned him too.). The lyrics tell the story of a Vietnam veteran who is treated badly back in the States.

And the cover art for the album of the same name? Annie Leibovitz took a lot of photos and, in the end, Springsteen thought the picture of his denim-clad rear end looked better than the ones of his face. Nothing symbolic or anything. While Springsteen does not allow his music to be used in advertisements, he allowed *Sesame Street* to do a parody called "Barn in the U.S.A."

The drum solo near the end of the recording was improvised by

E Street Band drummer Max Weinberg. The song was originally meant to be acoustic. Springsteen sometimes performed it that way, recognizing that the verses' lyrics were hard to understand in the recorded version.

Wind of Change

The video for Scorpions' "Wind of Change" shows the fall of the Berlin Wall, but the song itself was inspired by earlier events. In 1988, the group became the first Western rock band to perform in the Soviet Union. They returned the next year for the Moscow Music Peace Festival and were pleasantly surprised by the changes they saw, a result of Gorbachev's policy of *glasnost*.

As Germans, Scorpions had a desire to show their Soviet audience that Germans could bring love and rock and roll instead of tanks and war. Later, they started singing a version of the song in Russian, and also in Spanish. The song includes references to places in Moscow: the Moskva is a river and Gorky Park is a 300-acre public park in the center of Moscow, named after author Maxim Gorky.

The intro to "Wind of Change" was supposed to be played on guitar, but singer Klaus Meine decided to whistle it instead. The record company wanted to cut the whistling out, but the band stuck to their guns and the whistling stayed in.

Smells Like Teen Spirit

The title does, in fact, refer to the popular brand of deodorant. A friend of Nirvana singer Kurt Cobain wrote on the wall when he was sleeping: Kurt smells like teen spirit. Evidently, Cobain was unfamiliar with the product name and thought it sounded like a good song title.

Many fans have spent hours trying to read between the lines and find the meaning of the song. Kurt Cobain gave several different explanations, including a concession that it was "made up of contradictory ideas" and "making fun of the thought of having a revolution." Drummer Dave Grohl said Cobain wrote the lyrics five minutes before singing them and believes they are largely meaningless.

Nirvana got tired of performing this song, and it was often requested. Since the riff was very similar to Boston's "More Than A Feeling," the band sometimes started off with "Smells Like Teen Spirit" and then played a bad cover of "More Than A Feeling." For a show in Argentina, the band brought a relatively unknown all-female group called Calamity Jane to open for them. The audience booed Calamity Jane and pelted them with projectiles, which angered Nirvana. They decided to play the show but do a horrible job as revenge. They played the riff from "Smells Like Teen Spirit" and then launched into an unknown song.

RANDOM FUN FACTS

1. "Tomorrow Never Dies" by the Beatles is based on the *Tibetan Book of the Dead*. You can hear a Mellotron, a sitar, George playing an Indian instrument called a tanpura, as well as seagulls—actually, no, there were no seagulls. They recorded Paul McCartney laughing and distorted the sound.

2. "Respect" was written by Otis Redding, but Aretha Franklin was the one to make it an anthem for black and women's rights. Redding's version was a plea for respect for a man who has been working all day. Franklin changed a few of the lines and added the backup singers (her sisters), making it a demand for respect for a strong woman who knows her worth.

3. "Carrie Anne" by the Hollies is about singer Marianne Faithfull, but Graham Nash was too shy to call the song "Marianne." Actress Carrie-Anne Moss was named after this song—she was born three months after its release.

4. Have you ever wondered what kind of name "Sloopy" is? The lady in question was Dorothy Sloop, a jazz singer and pianist. A high school kid wrote the song about her and sold it to Wes Farrell and Bert Bems, who recorded it in 1964. The following year, the McCoys turned it into a No. 1 hit.

5. "For What It's Worth" by Buffalo Springfield is not exactly a protest song. Inspired by the Sunset Strip curfew riots but not specifically about them. The song is a call for sanity, imploring listeners to stay cool, think about what's going on, and avoid violence.

6. Cover songs can be tricky, and most musicians screw them up. This was not the case when Jimi Hendrix recorded "All Along the Watchtower," a song written by Bob Dylan. Dylan himself considered Hendrix's version an improvement on his own and says that now, when he performs the song, he thinks of it as a tribute to Hendrix.

7. The room in Cream's "White Room" is...the lyricist's apartment. While the final song goes deeper than that— poet Pete Brown's depression, a hippie girl, and a relationship he was in—the room was just an apartment, not a metaphor or an institution.

8. Steppenwolf's "Magic Carpet Ride" is not about acid or any other drug. Lead singer John Kay's initial inspiration was the superior sound of his new stereo system, and he filled it in with other lyrics that sounded good with the melody.

9. John Fogerty of Creedence Clearwater Revival got the idea for "Bad Moon Rising" while watching the 1941 film *The Devil and Daniel Webster*, particularly an apocalyptic hurricane scene. The song was also a metaphor for the tumultuous atmosphere of the late '60s. The last line of the

chorus has been misheard as "There's a bathroom on the right." Fogerty himself often slips this line in when performing, sometimes gesturing to a nearby bathroom.

10. Cat Stevens's songs "Lady D'Arbanville" and "Wild World" are both about the same woman—actress Patti D'Arbanville, who was his girlfriend at the time. "Wild World" was their breakup song. Stevens, now called Yusuf, still performs a song with the music from "Lady D'Arbanville," but with different words, out of respect for his wife, who does not like his songs about old girlfriends.

11. Elton John fans wondering who "Levon" is may be disappointed to learn that the song was not based on a real person. Elton John's lyricist Bernie Taupin claims that the song is free-form writing with no deep meaning. Levon is the middle name of Elton John's son, who was born on Christmas Day, but this was in 2010. Another "name" song by Elton John is "Daniel." Bernie Taupin wrote this song after reading about a wounded Vietnam veteran who was unable to continue with his old life due to the unwanted attention he got back home. Taupin chose to write the song from the perspective of the soldier's younger brother, and had Daniel go to Spain because it rhymed with "plane."

12. Bart Simpson was right. "In-A-Gadda-Da-Vida" really was supposed to be "In the Garden of Eden." When the vocalist/keyboardist of Iron Butterfly wrote the 17-minute

song, he was quite drunk and slurred his words. Drummer Ron Bushy liked the slurred version, and the rest is history!

13. According to Aerosmith guitarist Joe Perry, the phrase "Walk This Way" came from a comic scene in the Mel Brooks film *Young Frankenstein*. The rest of the song has nothing to do with the movie—it's about a schoolboy having his first sexual experience with a (probably older) cheerleader.

14. "Don't Fear the Reaper" is not a glorification of suicide. Blue Öyster Cult guitarist Buck Dharma was reflecting on his mortality and the fact that he could die young, and he was also thinking about his wife and wondering if they would find each other in the afterlife.

15. "We Will Rock You" was written by Queen's guitarist Brian May. He wanted a song the audience could participate in. Being Brian May, he used his knowledge of physics to calculate the amount of delay in the recording to simulate the sound of a large group of people clapping and stomping.

16. "Walk Like an Egyptian" is one of the Bangles' most-loved songs—but not by the band. They considered themselves serious rockers and felt that "Walk," being a goofy song that they didn't write themselves, compromised that image. At least one Bangle wrote or participated in writing each of their songs, with the exception of "Walk Like an

Egyptian" and "Manic Monday," which was written by Prince (that's why it sounds like "1999").

17. Don Henley wrote "Dirty Laundry" about sensationalism in the news. The events that sparked the song were journalists' insensitivity in the coverage of John Belushi and Natalie Wood's deaths, and the press hounding Henley after a 16-year-old girl overdosed in his house.

18. If you try to find South Detroit, you'll end up in Canada. Steve Perry of Journey chose "south" for "Don't Stop Believin'" because it simply sounded better than any of the other cardinal directions.

19. The working title of "Total Eclipse of the Heart" was "Vampires in Love." It was all about vampire love and the power of darkness, and it was intended for Meat Loaf. But Meat Loaf ended up writing his own songs for the album he was working on, and "Total Eclipse of the Heart" went to Welsh singer Bonnie Tyler.

20. Like "Born in the U.S.A.," Neil Young's "Rockin' in the Free World" is often falsely thought to be a patriotic song. It was a critique of the simultaneous consumerism and economic inequality in American society, and the lyrics censure the first Bush administration for breaking campaign promises.

21. "Shiny Happy People" by R.E.M. was meant to be ironic. Singer Michael Stipe got the idea for the title and chorus

from a Chinese propaganda poster, and he wanted to show the contrast between the poster and the events in Tiananmen Square.

22. Some listeners think Tom Petty's "Mary Jane's Last Dance" is about marijuana. While Heartbreakers' guitarist Mike Campbell says that listeners should feel free to form their own opinions, the name "Mary Jane" wasn't originally in the song. It was "Indiana Girl." Petty later said that Mary Jane and the subject of "American Girl" are the same character.

23. While the video for L.A. Guns' power ballad "The Ballad Of Jayne" features a waifish, dark-haired girl who may be a ghost, the song is about '50s blonde bombshell Jayne Mansfield.

TEST YOURSELF – QUESTIONS AND ANSWERS

1. Which song was written to vindicate and illustrate the genius of a famous artist?

   A) "Art of Dying" (George Harrison)

   B) "Painter Man" (The Creation)

   C) "Vincent" (Don McLean)

2. Which song was written for tennis star Billie Jean King?

   A) "Philadelphia Freedom" (Elton John)

   B) "Don't Stop" (Fleetwood Mac)

   C) "We Are the Champions" (Queen)

3. Which historical figure is *not* mentioned in Billy Joel's "We Didn't Start the Fire"?

   A) Joe DiMaggio

   B) The Rosenbergs

   C) Lyndon B. Johnson

4. "Silent Lucidity" by progressive-metal band Queensrÿche is:

   A) A lullabye

   B) A song about lucid dreaming

   C) A song about a nightmare

5. Ann Wilson of Heart thought this song, written by an outside lyricist, was disgusting and stopped singing it:

A) "Crazy on You"

B) "All I Wanna Do Is Make Love To You"

C) "Little Queen"

ANSWERS

1. C
2. A
3. C
4. B
5. B

CHAPTER FIVE

UNFORGETTABLE CONCERTS

Events like Woodstock brought music lovers together and made headlines—for good and bad reasons. Learn some facts about some of the most notable concerts in rock history!

Moondog Coronation Ball

The first rock concert took place on March 21, 1952, but it was a short one. Alan Freed, the radio host who coined the phrase "rock and roll" to describe the new musical forms, decided to organize a live dance event in the Cleveland Arena, which had a capacity of a little over 10,000 people. Due to circumstances probably involving a printing error and counterfeiting of tickets, around 20,000 people showed up and tried to crowd in. The fire marshal and the police department had to shut down the concert after less than an hour and disperse the crowd.

The next evening, during his show, Freed issued a public apology and invited listeners to call in and tell the operator whether or not they were with the Moondog Show. The support poured in. Freed later organized other concerts, including the Moondog Maytime Ball.

The program of the Moondog Coronation Ball had featured a number of black musicians who were popular with black and white listeners of Alan Freed's radio show: the Dominoes, who were just starting their careers and would be big throughout the '50s; Tiny Grimes, an R&B and jazz guitarist; Paul Williams and the Hucklebuckers, pioneer of the honking tenor saxophone solo; and singer Varetta Dillard.

The Ed Sullivan Show

From 1948–1971, entertainment columnist Ed Sullivan hosted a variety show, originally called *Toast Of The Town*, on CBS. Most people remember the show as the beginning of Beatlemania, but Sullivan hosted many other up-and-coming rock stars as well. The show appears on *TV Guide* Magazine's list of the 60 Best Series of All Time, coming in at #31 in 2013.

Let's start with the episode that started the British invasion: the Beatles' first performances on the show in February of 1964. The Beatles agreed on three performances in return for payment of their travel expenses. An estimated 38% of the U.S. population watched the show on television. Other statistics show that 60% of U.S. televisions that were turned on at that time were turned to CBS—Ed Sullivan and the Beatles.

The studio had a capacity of 703, but more than 50,000 people begged for tickets for the February 9th show. Richard Nixon's teenage daughter, Julie, was in the audience, but many other celebrities, such as Leonard Bernstein, were unable to get seats for their kids.

The Beatles were known for their cheeky humor. They were mobbed by journalists when they arrived at the Kennedy Airport. When asked how he found America, Ringo answered, "Turn left at Greenland." The frenzy didn't stop when they got to the hotel, as some teens pretended to be hotel guests in an attempt to meet the band. Fans knew exactly where the Beatles would be at any given time because Capitol Records had broadcast their itinerary on the radio.

The Beatles were the first performers at their February 9th debut, but they weren't the only acts. The Monkees weren't there, but Davy Jones was—the cast of Broadway's *Oliver!*, in which Jones played the Artful Dodger, performed songs from the play that night. He was nominated for a Tony award for his performance in *Oliver!* and went on to have a successful career. Not all of the other acts fared so well. Charlie Brill and Mitzi McCall, married comedy duo and future godparents to Melissa Gilbert, encountered a highly distracted audience and became distracted themselves, forgetting some of their lines and giving a subpar performance. They later said it ruined their career. Sullivan had tried to keep the fans' enthusiasm for the Beatles under control, threatening to "send for a barber" if they didn't behave. Another guest was the Riddler from the *Batman* TV series starring Adam West. Aside from his Riddler persona, Frank

Gorshin was a popular impressionist who made audiences laugh by impersonating other stars, such as Marlon Brando.

Before the Beatles' performance, Sullivan read a telegram of congratulations from Elvis to the Beatles, but Elvis didn't write it. His manager did, in the hopes of making Elvis look good. The Beatles performed five songs over their two acts that evening: "She Loves You," "All My Loving," "I Wanna Hold Your Hand," "Till There Was You," and "I Saw Her Standing There." When the camera focused on John, the caption read, "SORRY GIRLS, HE'S MARRIED."

George Harrison almost missed it. He'd come down with tonsillitis and had to skip the rehearsals, but was determined to get through the actual performance, though he had a fever of 102. Some attendees claimed that the studio had a strong smell—of urine. Evidently, the excitement was too much for the bladders of some adoring fans. Other attendees claim that this was a mean-spirited urban myth spread by jealous males. Allegedly, John was intrigued by the vending machines in the studio and asked the stage producer for change so he could try them out. The Beatles' second appearance on *The Ed Sullivan Show*, on February 16th, didn't take place in the Ed Sullivan Theater, but at The Deauville Hotel in Miami Beach.

The Beatles' appearance may be the most famous, but the Dave Clark Five had more performances than they did—they appeared on the show 18 times, more than any other British group. Nine years before the Beatles' appearance, Bill Haley & His Comets performed "Rock Around the Clock" on *The Ed Sullivan Show*. The CBS network, music historian Jim Dawson, and others considered this to be the first rock performance on national TV.

In 1956, a reluctant Ed Sullivan invited Elvis to perform. He had initially objected to having the singer on his "family show" because of his provocative hip gyrations, but he had to give in after several competitors featured Elvis on their shows, probably resulting in higher ratings. Elvis appeared three times; his first two shows were "uncensored," but on his third appearance, he was only filmed from the waist up.

The Supremes were a particular favorite of Sullivan's, and they appeared on the show 14 times (or 15, depending on how you count them). The Ed Sullivan Show invited a number of black artists through the '50s, against the initial wishes of some sponsors, and Sullivan claimed tha "we've put on everything but bigotry" (whether or not his actions always reflected those words).

Finally, various Muppets have performed on the show 25 times. The Ed Sullivan Theater today is probably best known as the home of *The Late Show with Stephen Colbert*.

Newport Folk Festival

Newport, Rhode Island is home to the Newport Folk Festival, founded in 1959. Several notable folk/rock musicians have performed there, such as Bob Dylan, Pete Seeger, and Joan Baez. It is one of North America's first modern music festivals. Joan Baez made her debut the first year. The second year, the festival was expanded and included folk musicians from all over the world.

This was where the song "We Shall Overcome" became a staple of the Civil Rights Movement. It was based on an older Baptist hymn, "I'll Overcome Some Day." Theo Bikel and the Freedom Singers, Joan Baez, Bob Dylan, and Pete Seeger performed the new version as the last act on the Friday of the 1962 festival. Participants also integrated a bus in the '60s when a group of white performers stopped to pick up a group of black performers. The bus was already full, so the white male performers stood up to allow the black female performers to sit.

At the 1965 festival, Bob Dylan caused controversy for using an electric guitar. There are two accounts for the source of the audience's discontent. One story, supported by Pete Seeger, is that audience members were booing simply because the sound system was bad and they couldn't hear Dylan properly. The other story is that some folk purists felt that Dylan was "selling out" by using an electric guitar instead of an acoustic one, therefore merging rock and folk. He also had a nine-piece band backing him. However, he wasn't the first folk musician to play an electric guitar at the festival; the Butterfield Blues Band, the Chambers Brothers, and Howlin' Wolf had performed with electric guitars that year, and Muddy waters had always used one.

The Beatles at Shea Stadium

The first stadium rock concert took place on August 15th, 1965 when the Beatles performed for a crowd of 55,600 mostly teenage fans at Shea Stadium, home of the New York Mets baseball team. It was the start of the band's second U.S. tour. Tickets cost $5.65 including tax, and the concert brought in $304,000. The band got $160,000.

New York City authorities nixed the Beatles' idea of landing on the diamond by helicopter, so they arrived in a Wells Fargo armored van. They did, however, get a tour of the city by helicopter before the show. The tour and show were filmed by Sullivan Productions.

The stage was far from the audience, on second base, and only police and security were allowed on the infield. There were 2,000 security personnel for the concert. A few fans fainted and had to be carried out. The distance from the audience did save the band from being pelted with jelly beans, though. Vendors sold cheap binoculars and Beatle wigs. Fans held banners and wore sandwich boards, one of which read, "Paul, Don't Marry

Jane" (actress Jane Asher broke up with him in 1968).

Shea Stadium was closed in 2008. To bring things full circle, Paul McCartney, along with Billy Joel, played the last concert there.

Fantasy Fair and Magic Mountain Music Festival

This was the first event of the famed Summer of Love and the prototype of modern outdoor rock festivals. It was scheduled for June 3rd and 4th of 1967, but bad weather forced the organizers to postpone it one week. It took place on Mount Tamalpais in Marin County, California, at the Sidney B. Cushing Memorial Amphitheatre. Since the festival was organized by the KFRC radio station, it is often referred to as the KFRC Festival.

The mountain is in the San Francisco area, which was the center of the hippie counterculture at the time. While rock started out as the music of teenagers, with the Beatles, Elvis, and other acts, it was now firmly a part of the adult scene, with psychedelic rock on the rise. Audience members traveled up the mountain by school bus.

Tickets cost $2.00 and organizers donated the proceeds to Hunters Point Child Care Center in San Francisco. It was a multi-act outdoor festival that included a number of rising musicians: the Doors, Canned Heat, Dionne Warwick, Jefferson Airplane, the Byrds with South African trumpeter Hugh Masekela, the Seeds, the Grass Roots, Country Joe and the Fish, among many others, for a total of over 30 acts.

A co-producer claimed that the Grateful Dead's "chemist" distributed acid into the crowd. The organizers took the precaution of bringing a doctor to handle people who had "bad trips" (which included some performers, such as Don Van Vliet of Captain Beefheart & the Magic Band). There were tire swings for guests to use, as well as a "toboggan" slope of wet straw to slide down on a piece of cardboard.

The Byrds didn't have a drummer with them. A member of the stage crew offered to drum for them, but there were no spare drumsticks available, so he cut off the legs of a coffee table and used them. Since there was no backstage area, the musicians mixed freely with the crowd. It was the first large show for the Doors. Jim Morrison made a great impression on the crowd as a musician while singing "Light My Fire," but not as a person, as he was drunk (evidently, people who were high looked down on people who were drunk) and fell off the stage during the performance.

Newspaper accounts say the participants behaved well and left the premises clean.

Monterey International Pop Music Festival

The Monterey Pop Festival was more publicized than the KFRC festival of the previous week, and it took place at the Monterey County Fairgrounds in California, from June 16th to June 18th,

1967. It was a much larger festival, with the crowd size fluctuating between 25,000 and 90,000 people.

The ticket price for the full weekend was $6.50, but attendees could also purchase tickets for one day. Most of the musicians performed for free and only accepted payment for travel and accommodation. Ravi Shankar got $3,000 for his sitar performance. Shankar performed for an afternoon, but other artists got 40 minutes, with some performing for 25.

Though Jimi Hendrix was well known in the United Kingdom, most people in the U.S. still had not heard of him. That changed at Monterey. His proficiency on the guitar was unparalleled, and he even played it behind his back and plucked the strings with his teeth. After playing "Wild Thing," Hendrix lit his guitar on fire before smashing it and throwing the pieces into the audience. Hendrix knew he had to one-up the Who. They had played before him and were known in the U.K. for smashing their instruments.

Other notable performances included Otis Redding, who hadn't played for many large white audiences before, and Janis Joplin's rendition of "Ball and Chain" with Big Brother and the Holding Company. Some musicians were unable to come because they couldn't get a visa: the Kinks, Donovan, and the Rolling Stones. The Beach Boys also canceled.

Flowers were everywhere, even on police officers. About 100,000 blossoms were brought from Hawaii and given to guests. Hippie culture was relatively unknown outside California until Monterey, when footage of the festival was broadcast on national TV. The quintessential hippie song "San Francisco (Be Sure To Wear Flowers In Your Hair)" was composed specially for the occasion by John Phillips of the Mamas and the Papas, to be sung by Scott McKenzie at the close of the festival.

The Beatles' Rooftop Concert

The Beatles' final public performance was a surprise. On the roof of their multimedia corporation, on January 30, 1969, the band treated an office and fashion district in central London to an impromptu performance, playing for 42 minutes before police asked them to keep quiet. Parts of the performance can be seen in the documentary *Let It Be*.

The Beatles couldn't be seen well from the street, but a crowd of people, mostly on their lunch break, formed to listen. Office workers leaned out of their windows to enjoy the performance, and workers in neighboring buildings watched from their roofs. Traffic stopped.

The performance also involved women's clothing. John and Ringo must have forgotten it was winter, and they didn't have their jackets. Ringo wore his wife's candy-apple-red raincoat and John wore Yoko Ono's fur coat. Since the wind was causing mic noise, an engineer covered the microphones with pantyhose.

Aside from the Beatles' own songs, they sang parts of "Danny

Boy" and "God Save the Queen." After closing the set with made-up lyrics to the tune of "Get Back" (the police were up there), John ended by saying, "I'd like to say thank you on behalf of the group and ourselves, and I hope we've passed the audition."

The Beatles were not the first to hold a rooftop concert, however; Jefferson Airplane had done so the month before in New York, and were stopped by police after one song. While the police did stop the Beatles' performance, they waited quite a while to do so. The police department was meters away from the Beatles' Apple headquarters. They only came after a few business people started complaining.

As this performance took place at a time when the Beatles were fighting amongst themselves (they would break up soon after), they hired a sessions keyboardist—American musician Billy Preston—as a buffer. It worked. The building that once housed Apple corps. (not to be confused with the computer company) and was the home of the rooftop concert is now an Abercrombie & Fitch.

Woodstock

Everyone's heard of the Woodstock Music & Art Fair. Did you know it didn't take place in Woodstock? The original plan was to have the event near that town, but they ended up changing the location several times due to lack of suitable venues and permits. Dairy farmer Max Yasgur allowed the organizers to use the fields where he grew alfalfa for hay (not his actual dairy farm).

August 1969 was two years after the Monterey Pop Festival, and the performers from that festival were now big stars. Rainy weather caused timetable disruptions, so that many bands ended up performing hours after their scheduled times. Jimi Hendrix started his famous performance, which included his psychedelic rendition of "The Star-Spangled Banner," at 8:30 Monday morning, when the 400,000-person crowd had dwindled to 30,000.

Actually, traffic threw the schedule off even before the rain came. Richie Havens was scheduled to perform in the evening, but the opening acts didn't arrive on time and he had to take their place. Havens had to fill the time until other bands got there, so he played everything he knew and then started on "Freedom." The thing is, this wasn't a song yet—he improvised it on the spot and had to watch the video later to remember what he'd sung! Havens died in 2013 and his ashes were scattered at the Woodstock festival site.

It wasn't intended as a free concert. Tickets were sold for $18 or $24, but when the day came, organizers had to declare it a free concert since there had been no time to build a fence or ticket booths—with just a few days to plan after finally finding a venue, it was either the fence or the stage, and organizers wisely chose the stage.

Ravi Shankar didn't particularly enjoy his time at the festival, calling it "terrifying" and saying that the people in the mud reminded him of water buffaloes. Some bands missed the event. Iron Butterfly was stranded at the airport (and may have received an off-color telegram in response to their requests for a helicopter). Joni Mitchell was scheduled to appear on *The Dick Cavett Show* and her manager talked her into keeping that appointment. John Lennon claimed his visa request was refused. The Doors, Tommy James and the Shondells, and the Byrds later regretted their decision not to participate, claiming they didn't know it was going to be such a big deal. The frontman of Jethro Tull didn't like the idea of playing for so many high and naked people. And the guitarist of Procol Harum didn't want to miss the birth of his baby.

One woman was airlifted when she went into labor, and she gave birth in a nearby hospital, and another woman gave birth in a car. Many people say they were conceived at Woodstock. Due to insufficient preparation, vendors ran out of food quickly, leaving thousands of hungry hippies. A Bethel woman named Leni Binder made hundreds of peanut butter and jelly sandwiches for Woodstock attendees. The local Jewish community also made hundreds of sandwiches with cold cuts and pickles. Who distributed these sandwiches? Nuns. The U.S. military also airlifted food into the venue and provided up to 45 volunteer medics, despite the anti-war protests and songs.

Even with the crowds, the lack of food and facilities, and the mud, there was only one reported act of physical violence, and that took place onstage. Pete Townshend conked activist Abbie Hoffman on the head with his guitar when the latter interrupted the Who's concert. The activist left the scene and the show went on. Also, a concession stand was burnt down after raising its prices, a move deemed by attendees to be against the spirit of the festival. Even with the relatively good behavior, the organizers were plagued by 80 lawsuits, mostly from surrounding farms who hadn't expected the crowd. Since Woodstock cost much more than it brought in, they had to wait for the Woodstock film revenue to pay off their debts.

Isle of Wight Festival

Often called the "British Woodstock," the Isle of Wight Festival took place in England from 1968-1970, and it was restarted in 2002. While the 2017 ticket price was £195, it was only £1.25 in 1968. An act of parliament was named after the festival; the "Isle of Wight Act" prohibits gatherings of over 5,000 people on the small island without a permit. This was a result of the 1970 festival, which brought in over 600,000 people (some accounts say 700,000).

The 1969 festival marked the first performance Bob Dylan gave after a serious motorcycle accident he'd had three years before. In fact, he missed Woodstock because he was preparing to leave for this festival, which he especially wanted to attend because the island had been the home of Alfred Lord Tennyson. He also told promoters that he would only come if Richie Havens was also invited (he was).

Jimi Hendrix had his second-to-last performance at the festival in 1970 (His last concert was at the Open Air Love and Peace Festival in Fehmarn, Germany.), and he died three weeks later. Having performed "The Star-Spangled Banner" at Woodstock, he did "God Save the Queen" at the English festival.

Harlem Cultural Festival

This was a series of six concerts held on Sundays throughout the summer of 1969, and it is often called "Black Woodstock." The Black Panthers provided security, as police refused to do so. There were no incidents, even though 100,000 people attended the concerts.

Nina Simone sang her rendition of the Beatles' "Revolution," with quite a few lyric and stylistic changes. Simone later left the U.S., feeling that black people would never "get their due." The concerts were recorded, but no TV stations were interested in buying the videos. Aside from Nina Simone's performance and a few other clips, the footage has not been shown. The fact that such an important event has not been picked up by TV probably proves Simone's sentiments right.

Sly and the Family Stone performed at Woodstock and the Harlem Cultural Festival. Other performers included B.B. King, The Staples Singers, Mahalia Jackson, Gladys Knight, Hugh Masekela, and Stevie Wonder.

Altamont Free Concert

The Altamont Speedway Free Festival is often called the "anti-Woodstock," the end of the '60s, and the (second) day the music died. Accounts differ on exactly what happened there, but the fact is that a teenager ended up dead at the hands of a Hells Angel. In addition, there were three other accidental deaths and several acts of violence toward performers and other attendees, some involving Hells Angels. Previous events such as Woodstock, the Harlem Cultural Festival, and the Monterey Pop Festival had told the world that young people could achieve peace if given the freedom to do so, and Altamont seemed to end that idea.

Like Woodstock, the venue was changed, and the organizers (members of Jefferson Airplane and the Grateful Dead) were offered Altamont Speedway just 20 hours before the concert. Grace Slick stated that "the vibes were bad." She didn't feel good about the location but felt she had to accept it. The tour photographer, Ethan Russell, also reported a bad feeling about the area. (Later, astrologists would claim that it had been an inauspicious day for a concert.)

After the Hells Angels knocked out a member of Jefferson Airplane (Marty Balin), the Grateful Dead refused to perform and left the premises. The violence only stopped during the performance by country/rock band the Flying Burrito Brothers.

At least one woman gave birth at the festival (some accounts say four).

There were 300,000 people in attendance, with no water or bathrooms. Local police and residents had not been informed of the concert. The stage was low and, therefore, easy for people to climb onto who weren't supposed to be there. The Hells Angels, who were there to provide security through intimidation, had taken their payment in beer and were drunk. It was a recipe for disaster and a blueprint for how *not* to plan a concert.

Strawberry Fields Festival

Like other festivals, the venue was changed several times. It ended up at Mosport Raceway in Bowmanville, Ontario. In Canada, this 1970 event was advertised as a motorcycle race with contemporary entertainment in an attempt to avoid public outcry against a rock concert. Since it was openly advertised as a rock concert in the U.S., locals soon found out what it really was, but the Supreme Court allowed it to proceed. To avoid making liars out of the organizers, a few motorcyclists took some laps around the track during the event.

John Lennon and Yoko Ono were supposed to host the event, but they backed out after the first change of venue. Attendees did not report many notable performances at the festival, but they had fun lounging in the sun and skinny dipping in the lake.

The one exceptional performance was when Sly and the Family Stone closed the event by playing "I Wanna Take You Higher" as the sun rose.

Since "Love, Sun, and Sound" had been so heavily promoted across the border, thousands of Americans hit the road and headed for Canada. Several were turned back because they couldn't prove they had sufficient funds (about $40) to support themselves there. One fan drowned in an attempt to swim the St. Lawrence River. Others were arrested for carrying illegal drugs.

Glastonbury Festival

This annual festival in Somerset, England has seen some great performances. As of 2015, the festival has welcomed over 2.8 million people and made £325 million. The first festival took place in 1970 and attendees got free milk from nearby farms with their £1 ticket. Most attendees camp there. In 2015, £8,995 could get you a tent with four bedrooms, a butler, and three bathrooms. You can book a yurt, too, if that's your fancy. If you live in the nearby village of Pilton, don't worry. You get a free ticket!

Glastonbury started off small. In 1970, 1,500 people attended. It was the day after Jimi Hendrix died. In 1971, the mystical-minded producer, Andrew Kerr, scheduled the festival over the solstice. He also used sacred geometry to choose the

Glastonbury site and had the pyramid-shaped stage built as a sacred structure.

There wasn't supposed to be a festival in 1978, but 500 people turned up on their way from Stonehenge, thinking there was one. They set up an impromptu festival powered by a generator, and some bands who happened to be nearby came to play. There were no huge names: Sphynx and a space rock band called Hawkwind.

It became an annual event in 1981, with a few short breaks. Because it often rains at that time, mud sports, such as mud surfing, became popular. In 1984, attendees got into the *Guinness Book of World Records* for a feat that had nothing to do with music. 826 people juggled 2,478 objects in total! Organizers in 2007 were well prepared, with 2,485 miles of toilet paper on hand!

Live Aid

By 1985, organizers of benefit concerts had learned a lot, and the management was much more efficient than George Harrison and Ravi Shankar's concert for Bangladesh. Live Aid was a global concert opened by Prince Charles and Princess Diana in London at Wembley Stadium. Over a billion viewers watched the 16 hours of music on TV or attended in London or Philadelphia. There were shows in Germany, Japan, the Soviet Union, and Australia, but they were not broadcast.

The goal was to raise money for Africans who were suffering under famine, and the concert brought in over $125 million. The singles "Do They Know It's Christmas" and "We Are the World" came before Live Aid, and raised over $54 million. Phone lines were set up to take donations. The royal family in Dubai donated £1 million. This was the largest donation.

The organizer, Bloomtown Rats singer Bob Geldof, was knighted for his work. However, this didn't help him find a taxi after the program, and he had to hitch-hike to get home. As for the musicians, there was one who played both concerts—thanks to Concorde, Phil Collins performed in London and then in Philadelphia. The concert was so big that all the rehearsal spaces in Philadelphia were booked and the Pretenders had to rehearse in a bar.

Eric Clapton got a shock from his microphone while performing "White Room." Geldof felt that the best performance of the event was Queen's, and he wasn't alone. The band went all out for Live Aid, seamlessly performing a medley of six hit songs. Since this was a tightly organized concert, all performers had to stick to a 20-minute time limit, and a red light warned them that their time was up. Pete Townshend, being Pete Townshend, broke the light and the Who played five more minutes.

U2 thought they'd given a poor performance, but it brought them into the mainstream. And Mick Jagger couldn't keep his, or his singing partner's, clothes on, first pulling off his own t-shirt and then ripping Tina Turner's dress, revealing a leotard. Perhaps they set a precedent for Super Bowl 2004. Live Aid wasn't free from controversy. Stevie Wonder noted that there were few black performers (Geldof then added more). Also, unbeknownst to most viewers (and probably the organizers and performers too), the biggest problem in Ethiopia was not famine, but civil war, and some of the money may have ended up financing the dictator.

Lollapalooza

Lollapalooza, an annual music festival featuring heavy metal, alternative rock, punk, and hip hop, among other genres, was originally organized by Jane's Addiction singer Perry Farrell. From 1991-1997 and in 2003, Lollapalooza was a traveling festival, but poor ticket sales in 2004 ended this, as well as canceling the festival for that year. It now takes place in Chicago, and there are a few international branches.

The word "lollapalooza" means "an extraordinary or unusual thing, person, or event; an exceptional example or instance." It was also once a shibboleth, used by American soldiers during World War II, as Japanese spies would not have been able to pronounce it correctly. Farrell heard it in a Three Stooges film and liked the way it sounded.

The event indirectly spawned another festival. Ozzy Osbourne was initially rejected by Lollapalooza organizers for some reason (perhaps they didn't want any burning crosses or bat incidents). Ozzy's wife, Sharon, gave Ozzy his own festival—Ozzfest. This led to the reunion of Black Sabbath.

Mosh pits and crowd surfing became popular in Lollapalooza. The festival also featured open-mic tents, tattoo artists, and piercing parlors. After the show settled in Chicago, Kidzapalooza opened its own area next door, showing family-friendly performances.

In 1993, the four members of Rage Against the Machine took the stage wearing nothing but a strip of tape over their mouths, with the letters PMRC painted on their chests. This was a protest against the Parents Music Resource Center, a censorship project fronted by Tipper Gore. The audience at first cheered them on, then started throwing plastic water bottles when it became apparent the band wasn't going to perform at all.

Attendees at the 1995 festival decided to have fun with a mud fight. Unfortunately, it wasn't much fun for Pavement, the band that was performing at the time. When someone threw a handful of mud at guitarist Stephen Malkmus, singer Scott Kannberg flipped the bird and mooned the crowd before the band left the stage.

RANDOM FUN FACTS

1. When we talk about rock festivals, we mustn't forget that they existed outside the U.S. and U.K. The first rock festival in a communist country was called Parada ritma (parade of rhythm). It was the first in a series of concerts that took place throughout Yugoslavia in 1964 and 1965 and featured a number of bands such as Iskre (the Sparks), Safiri (the Sapphires), Lutalice (the Wanderers), and Zlatni Dečaci (the Golden Boys).

2. The Mantra-Rock Dance, held in January 1967 in San Francisco, forged a seemingly unlikely relationship between followers of the Hare Krishna Movement and rock music. Referred to as "the ultimate high," it brought together musicians, including the Grateful Dead and Janis Joplin, Indian swamis, the Hells Angels, and hippies. The festival led to a greater awareness of the Hare Krishna Movement and gave many hippies a viable alternative to drugs.

3. The Atlanta International Pop Festival took place a month before Woodstock. It was one of Led Zeppelin's first big concerts, and it was so hot that the fire department sprayed attendees with water.

4. On July 5th, 1969, the Rolling Stones gave a free concert in

Hyde Park—their first in two years. The performance began with a tribute to former band member Brian Jones, who had died two days before. Fans brought candles and Mick Jagger appeared in a frilly white dress and read part of a poem by Percy Shelley on the death of John Keats. Against park regulations, the band released hundreds of white cabbage butterflies. Jagger later tore off the dress.

5. The first known instance of concert attendees waving lighted matches or lighters during a performance occurred in September 1969, at the Toronto Rock and Roll Revival. Evidently John Lennon got stage fright before his appearance with the Plastic Ono Band, and the master of ceremonies asked everyone to "light up" to welcome him.

6. In 1970, the Who really wanted to release a live album. They booked shows at the University of Leeds and at Hull and had them both recorded. The tapes from Hull were unusable, but the recording from Leeds was perfect. They had played 38 songs for 2,000 fans on Valentine's Day, and the result was one of the best-selling albums of all time. Fans who were unable to get tickets sat on the roof to hear and feel the music, and Roger Daltrey said the Leeds crowd was the best audience they'd ever had.

7. Another successful live album was made by B.B. King in the Cook County Jail. Prisoners booed the officer who introduced the singer, but B.B. King launched into "Every Day I Have the

Blues," followed by a number of other songs, accompanying himself masterfully on his electric guitar. The audience was on their feet by the end.

8. Another word should be said about Jimi Hendrix's performance of "The Star-Spangled Banner" at Woodstock, described by the *New York Post*'s rock critic as "the single greatest moment of the 1960s." Woodstock had been full of anti-war protests and, though Hendrix himself never called his performance a protest or said much at all about its significance, people continue to have different opinions as to his intentions. Some saw, and see, his performance as a patriotic tribute while others hear a protest song: the distortions and embellishments used by Hendrix near the end (around the "bombs bursting in midair" part, to be precise) sound like bombs, gunfire, and possibly tanks and screams. Hendrix even managed to work some bars of "Taps" into the mix. Other analysts say the performance was both an act of patriotism and a critique: we can love our country but protest its injustices.

9. While today it is common for musicians to play a benefit concert to raise money for victims of a natural disaster, impoverished children, or refugees, there had to be a first. And that was the Concert for Bangladesh, organized by Ravi Shankar and George Harrison. Bangladesh had been hit by a cyclone, floods, and a devastating war, and the concert

raised about $12,000,000 (Shankar had originally hoped to raise $25,000). UNICEF then took the money and distributed food and clothing to the refugees.

10. Aretha Franklin gave one of the best live performances in history in March 1971 (actually, three live performances), resulting in the album *Live at Fillmore West* (now available as a four-disc set). As a soul and gospel singer, she was unsure of how the San Francisco hippies would receive her. She had the audience in the palm of her had from the beginning, with "Respect," and she went on to play a series of original songs and covers. Her original song "Dr. Feelgood" is usually cited as the best part of the performance, as well as when she dragged Ray Charles, who was there as a spectator and didn't plan on performing, onto the stage for a duet.

11. The Bath Festival of Blues and Progressive Music took place in June of 1970. Like Woodstock, it was plagued by rain and roads that were so congested that performers (and their equipment) were late. To keep the crowd busy, Scottish singer Donovan went onstage and sang "I know an old lady who swallowed a fly." Once the performers arrived, other notable moments followed, including a Led Zeppelin performance in which Jimmy Page played a guitar solo with a bow and Pink Floyd's suite with a complete brass band and choir.

12. At the Great Ngaruawahia Music Festival in New Zealand in 1973, eccentric Kiwi rocker Corben Simpson made headlines by stripping onstage. He hadn't planned to do so; he took off his shirt due to the heat and got carried away when audience members yelled at him to continue, until he was wearing nothing but his guitar. Festival attendees joyfully threw off their own clothes, and the performer was fined $500. Not to be outdone, Ozzy Osbourne burned a cross with the rest of Black Sabbath.

13. California Jam, a 1974 music festival, marked the first time a Goodyear blimp floated over a live show and also the first time a band arrived in their own plane: Deep Purple's painted jet, the *Starship*. They left in a hurry by helicopter, though. Notoriously temperamental guitarist Ritchie Blackmore was in a particularly testy mood that day, and he destroyed several guitars and threw a couple of amplifiers offstage into the audience. At the end of the performance, one gasoline-drenched amplifier exploded, setting the stage on fire, and the band hightailed it out to avoid the wrath of the fire marshal. Guitar fans may enjoy hearing that one guitar finally got its owner back in 1987, when Blackmore threw it into the air and it landed on his finger, breaking it.

14. The definitive recording of Bob Marley's "No Woman, No Cry" was made in 1975 at the Lyceum in London. Though

Marley at that time was more contemplative onstage, for this performance he got the audience involved, and the result was one of the best songs of all time.

15. In addition to rock music, attendees of Texxas Jam 1978 were treated to comedy: Cheech and Chong were there and performed between acts. Nine years after Woodstock, Texxas Jam featured a very different lineup: Ted Nugent, Van Halen, Eddie Money, Aerosmith, Journey, and Heart, among others.

16. From their first performance as the Grateful Dead on December 4, 1965 in San Jose, the iconic band put on some of the most memorable shows in rock history. In fact, they played 36,086 songs over 2,317 live concerts. They never minded fans taping their shows, often designating a special area for those who wanted to do so.

17. Apple co-founder and rock fan Steve Wozniak was great with computers, but not so great at budgeting for concerts. He organized the US Festivals (pronounced like the pronoun, not as initials) in 1982 and 1983 and booked mostly new wave and metal bands. By most accounts, the concerts went well and people enjoyed the festivities, but times had changed. The up-and-coming bands of the '80s charged huge fees to perform (Van Halen got $1.5 million in 1983) and, as a result, Wozniak allegedly lost $20 million in the venture. Evidently, Wozniak has no regrets.

18. Woodstock '94 was an attempt to recreate the original euphoria on the 25th anniversary of the first Woodstock. A few performers were the same: Santana, Joe Cocker, Crosby, Stills, & Nash, and Country Joe McDonald, among others. Aerosmith performed at Woodstock '94 but not at the original. They weren't a band yet in 1969, but Steven Tyler and Joe Perry attended the festival. Bob Dylan had declined the invitation to perform in 1969 but performed in 1994. In their second set, the Red Hot Chili Peppers all wore similar clothes to Jimi Hendrix's Woodstock outfit.

19. In frustration with the music industry's treatment of women, Canadian singer Sarah McLachlan organized the Lilith Fair. Disproving the idea that female acts were less profitable than male bands, the 1997 Lilith Fair played 38 shows and brought in $16 million. This was double the profit of Lollapalooza (which was heavy on male acts) at that time.

20. Though the performers at the Lilith Fair were all women (or bands fronted by women), there were men on the crew, and on the last day, Bonnie Raitt's tour manager bought them all sundresses. Men in sundresses made a surprise appearance onstage, forming a chorus line like the Radio City Rockettes.

TEST YOURSELF – QUESTIONS AND ANSWERS

---

1. This artist, who also contributed to the 1996 Romeo + Juliet movie soundtrack, performed at the Lilith Fair.

    A) Des'ree
    B) Garbage
    C) The Cardigans

2. Which phrase appeared on the promotion poster of the original Woodstock?

    A) Age of Aquarius
    B) An Aquarian Exposition
    C) Aquarius Lives

3. Which band was *not* known for destroying musical instruments?

    A) The Who
    B) Blue Öyster Cult
    C) Deep Purple

4. How did the Woodstock '94 poster differ from the original?

    A) There were two birds on the guitar neck, and the guitar was electric.
    B) The bird was blue to symbolize the change in musical style.

C) It featured a silhouette of a musician and guitar, and there was no bird.

5. Which former Beatle performed at Live Aid?

A) George Harrison

B) Ringo Starr

C) Paul McCartney

ANSWERS

1. C

2. B

3. B

4. A

5. C

CHAPTER SIX

AWARDS AND BROKEN RECORDS

We all love watching awards shows and hoping our favorite band gets recognized (unless you're one of those people who don't like when the band goes mainstream). Which singer has been inducted into the Rock and Roll Hall of Fame three times and which band was robbed? Who had Top 40 hits in four decades? Are any of your favorite singers in the *Guinness Book of World Records*? Read and find out!

Rock and Roll Hall of Fame

The ultimate rock throne room, where every musician wants to be. The site, Cleveland, Ohio, was chosen because it was the site of the Moondog Coronation Ball and it beat Memphis in a *USA Today* poll in 1986. The seven-level building is a museum with permanent exhibits dedicated to specific genres and artists, and they also host temporary exhibits.

The curators also added a list of "500 Songs That Shaped Rock and Roll," but it had to be changed to "The Songs That Shaped Rock and Roll" when they added new songs. The Beatles and the Rolling

Stones each have eight songs on there, more than any other artist.

Being Inducted

To get into the Hall of Fame, you have to do a bit of waiting. An artist will become eligible 25 years after releasing their first record. The first group was inducted in 1986: Elvis, Fats Domino, Chuck Berry, Ray Charles, Sam Cooke, Buddy Holly, James Brown, Little Richard, Jerry Lee Lewis, Robert Johnson, Jimmie Rodgers, the Everly Brothers, and Jimmy Yancey. Aretha Franklin was the first woman to be inducted, in 1987.

Many critics dislike the nomination and voting process, as the few individuals responsible are not musicians and may be giving the nominations based on their personal taste, and some critics suspect lobbying due to lack of transparency (they did recently introduce fan voting, which has helped). A bit of controversy surrounds the Monkees. Though they were influential as an early rock band, they are banned from the Hall of Fame because they started out as actors, not as an actual band.

Who's in There?

One artist has been inducted into the Hall of Fame three times— Eric Clapton, as a solo artist, with Cream, and with the Yardbirds. Artists who have been inducted twice include Paul Simon (solo and with Simon and Garfunkel), Neil Young (solo and with Buffalo Springfield), Michael Jackson (solo and with the Jackson 5), Jimmy Page (with Led Zeppelin and with the Yardbirds), and

David Crosby (with the Byrds and with Crosby, Stills, & Nash), among others. Each Beatle except Ringo Starr has been inducted solo as well as with the Beatles.

Band nominations can result in awkwardness. Some bands went through painful breakups and were not thrilled with having to be onstage together. This was the case with Heart—the Wilson sisters only reluctantly played a set with the Fisher brothers. Other bands have had changes in their lineup and discover that the Hall of Fame plans to include some former members and exclude others. Kiss refused to perform because the Hall of Fame only planned to induct the four founding members, excluding popular later members.

Disco group Chic has been nominated 11 times but never voted in. The Rock and Roll Hall of Fame has included rap acts in recent years: Public Enemy, Tupac Shakur, and N.W.A. In April 2018, Sister Rosetta Tharpe will finally be inducted as an early influence (because, in their definition, she predates rock). The five inductees as performers will be Bon Jovi, the Cars, the Moody Blues, Dire Straits, and Nina Simone.

The Grammy Awards

No, it's not named after your grandma—Grammy is short for "gramophone." It was almost called "Eddie," after Thomas Edison. The awards are assembled by hand in Colorado and are gold plated over a trademarked zinc alloy called Grammium.

Each statue weighs five pounds and two ounces. The trophies that the artists hold when accepting the award are not their actual trophies—they are "stunt" trophies. Artists will receive their actual trophies later, after their names have been engraved on them.

Like the Super Bowl, the televised Grammy Awards show is prime advertising real estate, and for good reason: Over 26 million people watched the show in 2017. But if you want to run a 30-second ad, it will set you back at least $1,200,000.

The Biggest Winners

The artist with the most Grammys, at 31, is not a rock musician. He was an orchestral and operatic conductor named Sir George Solti. As for rock stars, Stevie Wonder has won 25 and U2 has 22. Taylor Swift is the youngest artist to win a Grammy for Album of the Year. Since she probably doesn't fall under the "rock" category, you might also like to know that Alanis Morissette, who does fall under the rock category, is the second youngest to win that award, at age 21.

As for the most-honored albums, two rock albums are tied at nine Grammys each: *Supernatural* by Santana and U2's *How to Dismantle an Atomic Bomb*. And when the Queen of Soul, Aretha Franklin, is in the running for Best Female R&B Vocal Performance, no one else has a chance. She won the award eight years in a row, from 1968 to 1975, as well as three more times in 1982, 1986, and 1988! Lenny Kravitz achieved the longest streak for Best Male Rock Vocal Performance, at four years, from 1999-2002. And Michael Jackson and Santana are tied for most Grammys won in one night, at eight each.

And Those Who Refused

In 1991, Irish singer Sinead O'Connor became the first (and, so far, the only) musician to refuse a Grammy. She declined the award in protest of the increasing commercialization in the music industry. Sometimes winners end up in surprising categories. In 1989, everyone expected Metallica to win for Best Hard Rock/Heavy Metal Performance, but the award went to Jethro Tull, a band not considered by most to be a metal band. Frontman Ian Anderson didn't even attend the ceremony since he didn't expect to win. Chrysalis Records ran a congratulatory ad saying, "The flute is a heavy, metal instrument." Metallica did win the award in 1991, and drummer Lars Ulrich thanked Jethro Tull for not releasing an album that year.

Only one winner has had their award taken away, and that was Milli Vanilli, after word got out that they were not actually the singers of "their" songs. There are a number of much-loved artists who have never won a Grammy: the Who, Led Zeppelin, Jimi Hendrix, Bob Marley, Chuck Berry, the Grateful Dead and the Beach Boys. The Beatles were the first rock group to win a Grammy, for Best New Artist in 1965.

Billboard Charts

Billboard magazine tracks singles and albums by popularity, based on sales, airplay, and streaming. The Billboard Hot 100 tracks singles, and the Billboard 200 ranks albums.

Alternative rock band Imagine Dragons holds the record of Longest Run on the Hot 100 with "Radioactive," which stayed on the charts for 87 weeks and was the biggest rock hit of 2013. Cher went nearly 25 years between No. 1 hits: "Dark Lady" in 1974 and "Believe" in 1999. "Believe" stayed at No. 1 for four weeks.

As you already know, Pink Floyd holds the record of Longest Run on the Billboard 200 with *Dark Side of the Moon* (861 weeks!), but the Longest Reign on The Billboard 200 By A Man goes to Michael Jackson, for *Thriller*. That album stayed on the charts for 37 weeks and gave the King of Pop seven top 10 singles on the *Billboard* Hot 100. The Rolling Stones hold the record for the most top 10 albums—a whopping 36! However, the Monkees had four No. 1 albums in one year, in 1967.

Billboard also has a list of Top 100 Hits of All Time. As of 2015, four artists each have three songs on the list: Lionel Richie, Boyz II Men, Bee Gees, and Paul McCartney. And some songs just never hit No. 1. Foreigner held the No. 2 spot for ten weeks in 1981 and 1982 with "Waiting for a Girl Like You."

Several songs have debuted at No. 1, including "I Don't Want to Miss a Thing" by Aerosmith. The Beatles have had 20 No. 1 singles, and they also hold the record for most No. 1 singles in a calendar year: six in 1964 and five in 1965! They are also the only artist to have replaced themselves at No. 1 twice, for a total of three No. 1 hits in a row.

Guinness World Records

The *Guinness Book of World Records* needs no introduction. There are lots of rock-related Guinness records.

To achieve the Guinness record for Largest Performing Rock Band, the band in question had to be professionally conducted and be of a good standard. In 2016, Cui Jian, Father of Chinese Rock, conducted a 953-person rock band in Tianjin, China. The performers came from the Beijing Contemporary Music Academy and included 151 drummers, 154 guitarists, 101 bassists, 349 singers, 100 keyboardists, and 98 wind instruments! Many of the participants were children.

With all the talk of Woodstock, it was not the largest free rock concert. That award goes to Rod Stewart's New Year's Eve concert in 1994, on Copacabana Beach in Brazil. 4.2 million people attended the live show.

Even if you can't play guitar, you can play air guitar! 2,377 participants at the San Manuel Indian Bingo & Casino in Highland, California achieved the record for Largest Air Guitar Ensemble in

2011.

Not a rock musician, but Justin Bieber holds an unfortunate record. With over eight million "thumbs down" as of 2018, "Baby" is the most disliked video on YouTube. While we're on the subject of the internet, Miley Cyrus is the most searched pop star, beating the record set by Michael Jackson in 2009.

The record for First Gig on a Floating Iceberg goes to metal band The Defiled. Fans watched from fishing boats as the band played a 30-minute gig in the Greenland Sea. Speaking of ice, British singer Charlie Simpson did a concert in Oymyakon, Siberia, Russia for the record of World's Coldest Gig.

Sirs and Dames

A number of rock stars have been knighted. We've discussed Bob Geldof and Mick Jagger. But though Jagger is "Sir Mick," Geldof is not "Sir Bob." That's because he's Irish, not British. Instead of using the title "Sir," Geldof can add the initials KBE to his name (Knight Commander of the British Empire). Ravi Shankar's name also bears a KBE because of his influence on British musicians such as the Beatles. Another fun fact about Sir Mick is that Queen Elizabeth II had a doctor's appointment on the day of Jagger's knighthood, so Prince Charles did the honors. Speculations abound that the Queen thought Jagger was unworthy (Keith Richards agreed).

Both Paul McCartney and Beatles producer George Martin have

been knighted. Elton John received the honor in 1998 for music and charity work. Since Van Morrison is from Northern Ireland, not the Republic of Ireland, he holds the title of "Sir." Rod Stewart received the honors from Prince William, and Prince Charles knighted the Kinks' Ray Davies.

And Everyday People

While there are a number of Dames who are musicians, no female rock stars have been given the title.

Of course, some musicians have turned down an offered knighthood. Though he was known as the "thin white duke" for some time (not his best years, according to fans), David Bowie refused a knighthood, stating that he didn't know what it was for and that it wasn't what he had worked for. John Lennon returned his MBE (Member of the British Empire) in protest of British involvement in the Biafran war.

Record Label Wars

While there are a lot of awards out there for rock stars to get, sometimes a band's record label can damage them instead of helping them. Rocker Courtney Love published a long article on *Salon*'s website describing how record labels get so much more money from artists' music than the artists themselves.

Ann and Nancy Wilson of Heart wrote "Barracuda" in 1977 about the record industry, particularly its treatment of women. Their label, Mushroom, placed an article in a magazine as a publicity stunt, in which they implied that the Wilsons were not only sisters, but also lovers. The Wilsons did not know about this until someone asked Ann how her lover was. Ann wrote the lyrics in her hotel room, and Nancy wrote some angry music to accompany them. After Heart left Mushroom, the label released some songs that the band had not wanted to release.

Michael Jackson's feud with Sony is legendary, and Prince changing his name to an unpronounceable symbol was part of his conflict with Warner Bros. And Fantasy Records sued John Fogerty, saying he plagiarized...himself. They said his song "Old Man Down the Road" sounded too much like Creedence Clearwater Revival's "Run Through the Jungle."

Though relationships with record labels can be problematic, they do provide a level of security an independent musician doesn't have.

RANDOM FUN FACTS

1. Aerosmith has had Top 40 hits in four different decades, starting with "Sweet Emotion" in 1976. Their latest *Billboard* Top 40 hit was "Jaded," in 2001.

2. Under Mikhail Gorbachev's policy of *glasnost*, the first rock album to cross the iron curtain was Bon Jovi's *New Jersey*.

3. A number of artists have declined their Kennedy Center Honors in opposition to the government at the time of the offer, as the U.S. president customarily sits with the honorees.

4. Some artists changed their minds and decided to attend the Kennedy Center event in 2017 when they heard that President Trump would not be there. The Kennedy Center thanked him for not attending.

5. One of the most notable Kennedy Center performances took place in 2012, when the surviving members of Led Zeppelin were honored. Ann and Nancy Wilson of Heart performed "Stairway to Heaven," accompanied by Jason Bonham, son of late Led Zep drummer John Bonham.

6. Nick Cave declined his MTV Video Music Award nomination with a poetic twist: "My relationship with my muse is a

delicate one at the best of times and I feel that it is my duty to protect her from influences that may offend her fragile nature."

7. For some reason, the above-mentioned VMA awards have seen a lot of physical and verbal fights between musicians. Poison's Bret Michaels and C.C. DeVille had a fistfight in 1991, Axl Rose threatened to fight Kurt Cobain in 1992, Courtney Love threw makeup at Madonna in 1995, and the following year, David Lee Roth nearly fought Eddie Van Halen over a misunderstanding about whether or not Roth would be invited to rejoin the band.

8. Metallica became the first band to perform on all seven continents with a concert in Antarctica called "Freeze 'Em All." In the audience were scientists, as well as fans who braved the elements. The audience heard the performance through headphones, as traditional amplifiers could have damaged Antarctica's fragile ecosystem.

9. PETA named Anthony Kiedis of the Red Hot Chili Peppers the Sexiest Male Vegetarian Alive in 2008.

10. Vice President Hubert Humphrey wrote some of the liner notes for Tommy James and the Shondells' album *Crimson & Clover*. Humphrey invited 21-year-old Tommy James to be his presidential youth affairs adviser but then, of course, lost the election to Richard Nixon.

11. The guitar riff of "Smoke on the Water" has become a competition of sorts, as guitarists around the world try to top the Guinness record for the most guitars playing at once. The current record is 6,346, and the event was the annual Thanks Jimi Festival in Wroclaw, Poland. Deep Purple guitarist Steve Morse participated in this event.

12. Each year at the Thanks Jimi Festival, participants attempt to break their own record for the largest guitar orchestra playing Hendrix's hit "Hey Joe." Their current record is 7,356 guitarists, set in 2016 (there were only 6,299 in 2017).

13. "Turn! Turn! Turn!" was written by Pete Seeger, and it became the Byrds' second No. 1 hit. With nearly all the lyrics taken from the Biblical book of Ecclesiastics, it can be considered the world's oldest rock song.

14. When Redbone performed "Come and Get Your Love," they often started with a Native American "Fancy Dance" by guitarist Tony Bellamy. Redbone was the first Native American rock band to have a No. 1 hit.

15. The Grammy for Best Rock and Roll Recording was introduced in 1962, and it went to Chubby Checker for "Let's Twist Again."

16. Christopher Cross was the first to win a Grammy in each of the "Big Four" categories, in 1981, with his debut album

and song "Sailing." Norah Jones *almost* achieved the same feat in 2003, but she wasn't credited as the writer for "Don't Know Why."

17. A number of fan favorites have still not been inducted into the Rock and Roll Hall of Fame. A list of the most overlooked artists includes, near the top, Janet Jackson, Radiohead, Nine Inch Nails, Devo, the Smiths, and Soundgarden.

18. Eddie Vedder inducted the Doors into the Rock and Roll Hall of Fame in 1993, but he also filled in for Jim Morrison for the Doors' performance of "Light My Fire." He didn't sound like Jim, of course, but he did a pretty good job! (Although, for some reason, there was a rendition of "My Favorite Things" during the guitar solo.)

19. Elmo—that's right, the shaggy, red puppet—has won three Grammys! It was for best musical album for children, in 1999, 2000, and 2002.

20. Even stranger, another Grammy went to Bill Clinton, Mikhail Gorbachev, and Sophia Loren, for their collaboration on spoken-word children's album, Prokofiev's *Peter and the Wolf*!

TEST YOURSELF – QUESTIONS AND ANSWERS

1. Which musician turned down an induction into the Rock and Roll Hall of Fame?

   A) Sex Pistols

   B) The Velvet Underground

   C) Elvis Costello

2. Who holds the MTV VMA (Video Music Award) record for most awards in a single night?

   A) Nirvana

   B) Smashing Pumpkins

   C) Peter Gabriel

3. Which artist did *not* wear a butt-baring outfit to the VMAs?

   A) Lady Gaga

   B) Prince

   C) Marilyn Manson

4. Who has won the most American Music Awards (AMAs)?

   A) Elvis Presley

   B) Whitney Houston

   C) Michael Jackson

5. Which British band was nominated in 2018 for the Rock and Roll Hall of Fame but not chosen for induction?

   A) The Smiths

   B) Radiohead

   C) Eurythmics

ANSWERS

1. A
2. C
3. A
4. C
5. B

CHAPTER SEVEN

MAD MISCELLANY

Some stories and facts are just too crazy to fit into any category. Find out which singer had a crush on Ringo Starr and which band had an affinity for chainsaws! Learn about strange curses in the music world, who has been electrocuted by the equipment onstage, and which country's revolution may owe a debt to rock music.

Breaking up Is Hard to Do

As a fan, the worst news you can hear is that your favorite band is breaking up. Due to the intense pressure stars face when touring or playing long concerts, personality clashes, and changing musical directions, band breakups are a sad fact of rock music.

Yoko Ono is a common scapegoat for the breakup of the Beatles, but she wasn't really responsible for it. It's true, however, that she didn't get along with the rest of the band, especially George. Many accounts say that George and John got into a fight because Ono ate some of George's McVitie's chocolate digestive biscuits (Hey, they're good cookies!). Her presence in the recording studio annoyed the band because girlfriends and wives were previously banned from there, but her presence wasn't the only factor.

To put it briefly, John and Paul had very different creative approaches that sometimes harmonized and sometimes conflicted. Manager Brian Epstein's death meant the band had to handle the non-musical aspects (Apple lost them money since they weren't accustomed to budgeting), the new manager, Allen Klein, was a nightmare. George's songwriting abilities developed and he grew frustrated at being sidelined by John and Paul, and John's capriciousness added to the instability. The Beatles broke up in 1969 and all four band members went on to have successful musical careers on their own or with other bands.

Family Feuds

Sometimes band problems and family problems go hand in hand. Perhaps the most famous contemporary example is Oasis, led by brothers Noel and Liam Gallagher, who have never gotten along. Liam traces their rivalry back to a night he came home drunk and urinated on his brother's new stereo, and they fought their way through seven Beatles-inspired and drug-fueled albums before splitting for good in 2009. According to Noel, Liam smashed one of his (Noel's) guitars. Liam denied this, but Noel claimed he couldn't work with Liam any longer and that "He's like a man with a fork in a world of soup."

The Everly Brothers' personal conflicts were reinforced by abuse of prescription drugs and alcohol. The pot boiled over during a 1973 concert in Hollywood, when Don arrived drunk and botched the lyrics to "Cathy's Clown." Phil clobbered him with a guitar and the duo was broken. The most famous Kinks fight was between Dave Davies and drummer Mick Avory, but brothers Ray and Dave had their own rivalry, which culminated in Ray stomping on Dave's birthday cake.

Egos and Addictions

The Pixies broke up due to frontman Black Francis's jealousy over fans' love of bassist Kim Deal. Francis sidelined her, and Deal went on to form the Breeders. However, the biggest reason for band infighting and breakup appears to be the perception (or reality) that one or two people are assuming creative control over the band at the expense of other band members. This led to the demise of the Beatles, the Police, Smashing Pumpkins, Guns N' Roses, the Eagles, and Creedence Clearwater Revival. Substance abuse also killed important band members (John Bonham of Led Zeppelin) or rendered them unable to perform. In some cases, the band keeps going but never recovers its former glory.

Shortest Beatle Has a Long List of Fans

Though he has never been considered as handsome as his bandmates, Ringo Starr's humor, personality, and talent made him a favorite with fans, women, and other musicians. Legendary drummers Ginger Baker, Steve Gadd, Keith Moon, and John Bonham were all admirers of Ringo and raved about the Beatle's uniqueness and talent. Despite this, Ringo did not like to show off and, unlike many other drummers of his time, refused to do a drum solo lasting more than 15 seconds.

And Ringo was the one who inspired a streak of novelty records in 1964. Perhaps the most famous singer to record a song about Ringo was Bonnie Jo Mason, with "Ringo, I Love You." Never heard of her? Bonnie Jo Mason was the name Phil Spector gave to the teenage Cherilyn Sarkisian because her name didn't sound "American" or memorable enough. Still doesn't ring a bell? She later shortened her name and performed as Cher. The song didn't get much airplay, partially because her deep voice caused disc jockeys to think that she was a man singing about another man. And, well, this was the '60s. Other songs about Ringo include Pat Wyntyer's "Ringo, I Want to Know Your Secret," Rolf Harris's "Ringo for President, and "Ringo" by Lorne Green.

"Weird Al" Yankovic

The one-and-only Weird Al has been mentioned here a few times, but he really deserves his own space. Alfred Matthew Yankovic started playing the accordion when he was seven years old, and he can also play the keyboards and theremin (yes, the really difficult one). He follows a mostly vegan diet and has never done recreational drugs, though he had fun making his college acquaintances laugh when they were high.

Prolific Parodist

Weird Al has done over 65 parodies, but he also writes original songs. Most of his albums are half parody and half original. Legally, he doesn't need permission to write a parody of a song, but he asks anyway, in order to maintain good relations with record labels. Most artists like Weird Al and are happy to let him do the parody. Some, like Kurt Cobain, believe you've really made it when Weird Al parodies one of your songs. He recorded his first parody, "My Bologna" (from "My Sharona") in a bathroom on his college campus.

Generally, Weird Al does not accept suggestions from other musicians or fans, but there was one possible exception, as some say that "Like a Surgeon" was Madonna's idea. Michael Jackson was a fan of Weird Al and the two used to exchange notes when they recorded in neighboring studios. Jackson also allowed Weird Al to use the "Badder" music video set to record "Fat." Weird Al's highest-ranking hit today is "White & Nerdy," and Chamillionaire believed that Weird Al's parody boosted his own song and helped him win a Grammy.

No, Thank You

A few musicians did not want to be parodied, for various reasons. Due to his vegetarian diet and animal-rights activism, Paul McCartney did not want Weird Al to turn "Live and Let Die" into "Chicken Pot Pie" (McCartney suggested "Tofu Pot Pie"). Prince and Jimmy Page declined permission but didn't give reasons, though Page claims to be a fan. Weezer allowed Weird Al to use a snippet of "Buddy Holly" in "The Alternative Polka," but then changed their minds and asked a disappointed Al to remove it. Daniel Powter initially withheld permission for Weird Al to parody "Bad Day" with "You Had a Bad Date," but he changed his mind. Unfortunately, it was too late to record the song.

Weird Al also writes children's books. His first is called *When I Grow Up*, in which a young boy entertains his class with all the outlandish jobs he wants to have as an adult.

Shocking Performances

With all that electrical equipment onstage, something is bound to happen sometimes—and it has. Keith Richards reportedly flew backwards in a blue spark and ended up unconscious after his guitar touched a microphone stand (If you're a guitarist, learn how this works so it doesn't happen to you!). But apparently, Keith Richards is invincible, and he was fine soon after. George Harrison was also electrocuted by his microphone, but it was just a quick shock. Millennial pop star Kesha was electrocuted in a particularly sensitive body part by an electric "chastity belt" (do not try this at home).

Kiss guitarist Ace Frehley immortalized his brush with mortality in a song called "Shock Me," the first song he ever sang on an album. Still holding his guitar, the rocker grasped a metal rail and was promptly immobilized by the electric current. He finally managed to let go and fell several feet. He still finished the concert after a ten-minute break.

A Rock and Roll Revolution

Rock music helped Czechoslovakia usher in its nonviolent transition from communism to democracy. Plastic People of the Universe is a Czech rock band that, at its beginning, was influenced by the music of the Velvet Underground and Frank Zappa. Since the band had an English name and sang in English, rather than Czech or Slovak, and its members had long hair, all of which were seen as forms of protest against the then-communist government, the Plastic People had to perform underground and were eventually arrested in 1976.

A friend of the band's manager Ivan Jirous, Vaclav Havel, led a movement of dissidents who pioneered Charter 77, a manifesto that criticized the government for human rights abuses that went against the Constitution of Czechoslovakia. This movement of young people, in combination with Soviet-led initiatives through the 1980s of *perestroika* and *glasnost*, eventually led to the formation of a democratic government in Czechoslovakia. Vaclav Havel was elected president at the end of 1989.

This nonviolent transition was named the "Velvet Revolution" by the dissidents' English translator, Rita Klímová. The fact that the word used to describe the revolution is shared by the band "Velvet Underground" may or may not be a coincidence. Slovaks use the term "Gentle Revolution," and the word "velvet" may have been chosen by Czechs because velvet is a soft and gentle fabric. In any case, Lou Reed of the Velvet Underground visited Havel in his home in Prague Castle and met (and performed with) the Plastic People of the World.

Grunge Music

Grunge is a genre of alternative rock that began in Seattle in the mid-'80s but peaked in popularity in the mid-'90s. Alternative rock musicians sought to replace the increasing greed, ostentation, and ego they saw in the rock scene, particularly in glam metal, or hair metal. The term "grunge" is usually credited to Mark Arm, singer of the Seattle-based bands Green River and Mudhoney. He described the sound of his band at the time as "Pure grunge! Pure noise! Pure shit!" He later claimed that he heard this term used by Australian rockers to describe similar music.

Flannels and Boots Rule the Decade

Grunge music also influenced '90s fashion. Since many grunge musicians were from Seattle, where it is chilly and rainy, they wore clunky boots and flannel shirts. Hence, the popularity of combat boots and flannels in that decade. One of the biggest alternative rock bands is Pearl Jam. They originally called themselves "Mookie Blaylock," after the New Jersey Nets point guard of the same name, and though they didn't keep the name, they still dubbed their first album *Ten*, after his jersey number.

Nirvana was another influential band, but they broke up in 1994 after Kurt Cobain's death. Drummer Dave Grohl went on to form the Foo Fighters, but he almost joined Tom Petty and the Heartbreakers! Alice in Chains, one of the biggest Seattle grunge bands, was originally a hair band, though Layne Staley was the only member present in the band for both incarnations. They still have a connection to classic rock, though. Ann Wilson of Heart, also from Seattle, sings in three songs on the band's 1992 EP, *Sap*.

RANDOM FUN FACTS

1. The drink brand Snapple caught the attention of entomologists and music fans when they printed the following fun fact on one of their bottle caps: "Termites eat through wood two times faster when listening to rock music!"

2. The pest-control company Orkin tested Snapple's statement by placing miniature guitars in two tanks full of hungry termites, regaling the inhabitants of one tank with rock music and the other with softer tunes. The result? It's true! Termites in the "rock" tank likely ate faster due to the frequencies created by the rock instruments.

3. The Beatles' song "She Came In Through the Bathroom Window" was written by Paul about fans who really did sneak in the bathroom window. One woman entered Paul's home in that way before letting her friends in. They stole some of Paul's clothing and photographs.

4. A number of rising musicians have died at the age of 27, giving rise to the term "27 Club": Brian Jones, Jim Morrison, Janis Joplin, Jimi Hendrix, Ron "Pigpen" McKernan, Kurt Cobain, Kristen Pfaff, and Amy Winehouse, among others. The coincidence was noticed back in 1971, after Jim Morrison's death.

5. Four members of the 27 Club—Cobain, Morrison, Joplin, and Hendrix—had white lighters on them when they died.

6. Three members of Led Zeppelin have had horribly bad luck, leading some fans to speculate that the band was cursed after a rumored deal with the devil (which John Paul Jones allegedly did not participate in). John Bonham died of alcohol poisoning. Jimmy Page's heroin habit nearly killed him. Robert Plant was in a car accident with his family, leaving him in a wheelchair for some time. His young son died of a stomach infection.

7. In his later touring years, instead of trashing his hotel room, Robert Plant preferred to have a cup of tea or coffee and iron his own clothes to get himself in the mood to perform.

8. Leonard Cohen preferred whisky to tea and sang a Latin phrase, roughly translating to "I am poor, I have nothing," before his shows.

9. Guns N' Roses frontman Axl Rose avoids towns beginning with the letter "M" like the plague. This aversion intensified after one show he played with Metallica in Montreal in 1992. Metallica singer James Hetfield was badly burned by a piece of pyrotechnics and had to go to the hospital, cutting their set short. Rose, already rattled by earlier fiascos and bad sound quality, played a few songs with Guns N' Roses before panicking and hightailing it offstage and out of Montreal, leaving a stadium full of angry fans, who promptly started a riot.

10. Another musician rumored to have sold his soul to the Devil in exchange for success was blues singer Robert Johnson (also a member of the 27 Club).

11. Robert Johnson's song "Cross Road Blues" is widely believed to be cursed. Eric Clapton sang it shortly before his two-year-old son fell from a window to his death. Lynyrd Skynyrd covered it too, and half the band died in a plane crash. A surviving member, Allen Collins, was in a car crash in which his girlfriend lost her life. The Allman Brothers also performed the song, and two band members died in motorcycle accidents—one year apart and in almost exactly the same place.

12. Southern hard rock band Jackyl has a love of chainsaws. Lead singer Jesse James Dupree uses a gas-powered chainsaw as a musical instrument during the band's single "The Lumberjack." When performing, he also uses the chainsaw to cut up various pieces of furniture.

13. Jackyl prefers to play bars and backyard barbecues rather than arenas, and they set two Guinness records for playing 21 gigs in a 24-hour period and playing 100 concerts in 50 days (in 27 states). The former record has since been broken, but it's still pretty impressive.

14. Before the 1979 revolution, Iran had a thriving rock scene. The Godfather of Persian Rock, Kourosh Yaghmaei, received his first musical instrument at the age of *ten*—a

santour, a hammered dulcimer used in Persian classical music. He switched to guitar when he was 15 and had a string of psychedelic, progressive rock hits through the '70s. He released his latest album, *Malek Jamshid,* in 2016 via a Los Angeles-based label. Yaghmaei lives in Tehran, teaching guitar and writing stories for children.

15. The Doors' name comes from a novel by Aldous Huxley, called *The Doors of Perception.* Morrison had several nicknames, the most famous being the Lizard King. The line "I am the Lizard King, I can do anything" appears in one of his poems. Incidentally, when a Doors-loving paleontologist found a fossil of a giant lizard, he decided to name it after Jim—*Barbaturex morrisoni.*

16. There are some stories surrounding Iron Maiden's controversial album *The Number Of The Beast.* During recording, cold spots were reported in the studio and lights would flicker and go out for no reason. After the producer was involved in a car accident, he received a bill for £666.

17. Many Beatle children grew up to be musicians. Zak Starkey is a drummer and has worked with the Who and Oasis. Sean Lennon has released three solo albums. James McCartney plays guitar and drums. Dhani Harrison plays guitar in two bands and is as jaw-droppingly handsome as his dad!

18. But they're not all musicians. Julian Lennon once won a Grammy but appears to prefer photography. Jason Starkey

describes being Ringo's son as "a total pain." Mary Anna McCartney is a photographer like her mom, Linda.

19. Stella McCartney is a well-known fashion designer. Lee Parkin Starkey is also a fashion designer and a mother of triplets. Beatrice Milly McCartney is a teenager.

20. When *Nevermind* was released, Nirvana threw themselves a party at Rebar, a club in Seattle. However, they were all thrown out for having a food fight, allegedly involving a watermelon and ranch dressing.

TEST YOURSELF – QUESTIONS AND ANSWERS

1. A band made of musicians who are already famous from performing solo or in other groups is called a:

    A) Supergroup

    B) All-star group

    C) Megaband

2. Which artist initially disliked Weird Al's parody of their song?

    A) Coolio

    B) Lady Gaga

    C) James Blunt

3. The Czech band Plastic People of the World took their name from a song by:

    A) The Velvet Underground

    B) Ivan Jirous

    C) Frank Zappa and the Mothers of Invention

4. The only person to have been nominated for a Grammy, a Golden Globe, an Oscar, and a Nobel Peace Prize is:

    A) Sting

    B) Bono

    C) Bob Dylan

5. Alternative rocker Beck was offered the chance to compose music for which popular TV series? (He turned it down.)

   A) Breaking Bad
   B) Dexter
   C) Mad Men

ANSWERS

1. A
2. A
3. C
4. B
5. C

DON'T FORGET YOUR
FREE BOOKS

MORE BOOKS BY BILL O'NEILL

I hope you enjoyed this book and learned something new. Please feel free to check out some of my previous books on Amazon.